Teaching Literary Elements

by Tara McCarthy

SCHOLASTIC
PROFESSIONAL BOOKS

NEW YORK • TORONTO • LONDON • AUCKLAND • SYDNEY

Excerpt from *The Talking Earth* by Jean Craighead George. Copyright © 1983 by Jean Craighead George. Used by permission of HarperCollins Publishers.

Excerpt from *Where the River Begins* by Thomas Locker. Copyright © 1984 by Thomas Locker. Used by permission of Dial Books, a division of Penguin Books USA Inc.

Excerpt from *Call It Courage* by Armstrong Sperry. Copyright © 1940, The Macmillan Company. Copyright renewed © 1968 by Armstrong Sperry. Reprinted with permission of Simon & Schuster Books for Young Readers, an imprint of Simon & Schuster Children's Publishing Division.

Cover design by Jaime Lucero and Vincent Ceci
Cover illustration by Artville
Interior design by Solutions by Design, Inc.
Interior illustrations by Mona Mark

ISBN 0-590-20945-0

Table of Contents

An Overview of the Book

Rationale

As you know, there are three main reasons for presenting literary elements to your students:

INCREASED APPRECIATION AND ENJOYMENT OF LITERATURE

By exploring and delving deeply into the basic elements that go into all good stories (character, setting, plot), readers understand how each of these elements develops and builds upon others as a story evolves. The story thus becomes richer for readers.

INCREASED ABILITY TO CRITIQUE AND DISCUSS A PIECE OF LITERATURE

By learning and understanding the terms for literary elements (e.g., character, setting, plot, conflict, climax, resolution, imagery, dialogue), readers

❀ develop a common vocabulary for discussing and writing about books they've read.

❀ can focus directly on what particular aspects of a story they liked or disliked.

INCREASED ABILITY TO WRITE STORIES THAT SATISFY BOTH WRITER AND AUDIENCE

Through analyzing literary elements in books they're reading and enjoying, students "learn the ropes" that can enable them to write well-wrought stories of their own.

Format

A FLEXIBLE FORMAT FOR READING

The book is designed so that you can use it with students who have different backgrounds and experiences with reading literature.

STEP-BY-STEP. The first three sections of the book (Character, Setting, Plot) proceed step-by-step through the recognition of these basic elements. You may want to use this step-by-step procedure with students who have not yet studied literary elements per se.

PICK-AND-CHOOSE. With students who have a general awareness of literary elements but who need to fine-tune their understanding of these elements, you can find within the step-by-step procedure particular activities that such students can go to directly. Examples:

❀ Students may readily identify and describe main characters, but have some difficulty telling how they acquired this information. You may want to have these students go directly to Focusing on the Five Methods (page 17).

❀ Students may already know that a plot must proceed in logical steps, but have some difficulty identifying the conflict that sets the plot in motion. You may want to have these students go directly to How a Plot Is Developed (page 53).

ENRICH-AND-STRENGTHEN The fourth section of this book, Expanding the Reading and Writing Experience, can be used as:

❀ a start-up place for your reading "superstars" who already exhibit good understanding of the concepts of character, setting, and plot when discussing books and who seem ready to move on to finer distinctions such as point of view and theme.

❀ a follow-up place for all of your students as they master the essentials of character, setting, and plot.

A FLEXIBLE FORMAT FOR RESPONDING TO LITERATURE

The book provides a wide variety of ways for students to respond to literature. Examples:

Teacher-Student Dialogues	**Literature Circle Focuses**
Brainstorm Start-Up's	**Reader's Journal Ideas**
Visual Interpretations	**Free-Write Prompts**
Dramatic Interpretations	**Cross-Curricular Applications**
Hands-On Activities	**Partner and Small Group Ideas**

A FLEXIBLE FORMAT FOR WRITING

Students' own story-writing is not only a "proof-of-the-pudding" for you, the teacher (Does the student's story show a grasp of key literary elements?), but is also a way for students to have an exciting and personally rewarding writing experience (Does my story satisfy me and/or my audience?). Because students vary in their writing abilities, goals, and procedures, we've provided suggestions for different kinds of writing activities:

WRITE A WHOLE STORY. This can be the overall goal for most of your students. The steps for achieving the goal are incorporated in the writing-process steps in the first three sections of this book (Character, Setting, Plot).

DEVELOP JUST ONE OR TWO LITERARY ELEMENTS FOR A STORY. For many students, a realistic and rewarding goal may simply be to fully develop a character, to vividly describe a setting, or to make a coherent plot outline or plot-step for an original story.

JUST TELL YOUR THOUGHTS AND REACTIONS. Students may develop their understanding of literary elements through their free-writes/free-reads, their notes from Literature Circle discussions, their Journal entries, any visuals they've completed or any pictures they've drawn, and through their participation in acted-out stories.

Other Special Features in This Book

- ❀ **Excerpts from Great Literature for Young Readers**

- ❀ **Models of Teacher-Student Dialogues** provide hints about participating in your students' book talks.

- ❀ **Reproducibles** to help students organize their ideas about literature.

- ❀ **Assessment Tools** provide formats for students' self-assessment and for you to use with students.

- ❀ **A Glossary of Key Literary Terms** for you and your students to use as a reference.

- ❀ **An Annotated Bibliography**

Additional Ideas for Teaching Literary Elements

THE TEACHER AS A LEADER: TEACHER-STUDENT DIALOGUES

We've often been advised to let students conduct their own book talks and construct their own reactions to literature without teacher intervention. Such free-floating discussion may work well for a very few students. In general, however, we've noticed that most entirely teacher-free discussions of literature tend to get bogged down, side-tracked, or brought to unsatisfying, premature closure. Why? There's no leader to keep the discussion on track!

The leader in a book talk—whether it's between adults in a "literary salon" or between children in a classroom—is someone who (1) knows the book thoroughly; (2) has read similar stories; (3) aims for an essential outcome or understanding as a result of the discussion; (4) knows how to comment or question in order to keep the discussion on track; and (5) verifies and summarizes participants' on-target insights and encourages more of them.

We suggest that in your classroom this leader is you! The Teacher-Student Dialogues presented in this book provide examples of ways you can help students move toward essential understandings, such as the basic conflict a character must deal with or the descriptive phrases a writer uses to establish setting.

You might note and implement these <u>affective</u> qualities of a book-talk leader:

- ❀ The leader is involved personally with the story and is ready to share her or his personal reactions to it. For example, in discussing "Beauty and the

Beast," you can tell students how impatient or angry <u>you</u> got at Beauty's father or how you yourself—like Beauty—once had to make a difficult choice or figure out where your loyalties lay.

❀ The leader knows when to be nonintrusive. After setting the stage (e.g., how we may all in some way be like Mafatu in *Call It Courage*), the leader "backs away" and lets the other discussion participants build on the prompt.

❀ The leader senses when the dialogue is getting watered down or sidetracked and injects a personal comment or question to get the dialogue moving again in the desired direction.

❀ The leader senses when it's time to make a summary comment: the discussion participants have contributed the essential details that add up to the Big Idea, which the leader then presents. Example: "That was a scary decision that Beauty had to make. But as it turned out, she made the right one. I guess we all have to face scary decisions now and then."

As a savvy leader of book talks, your enthusiasm and focus will help your students gain great insights into literature. In addition, the model you set will help students understand how to critique and respond to literary elements.

STUDENTS AS THEIR OWN TEACHERS: WRITING IS "EVERYTHING"

The truism that's worth repeating is: "We learn to write through writing." (To this we can add: "We learn to <u>read</u> by writing.")

But in considering *how* people—young or old—go about writing, it's useful to consider two main approaches, both of which are encouraged in this book. The first approach, linear, is one <u>you</u> can teach. The second approach, recursive, is one that students can only teach to themselves, and then only if you allow them the time and space to do so.

1. The Linear Approach

The linear approach is very "teachable" because it proceeds in orderly steps. As students learn about literary elements, they have several opportunities to use one or more of the traditional writing-process steps—drafting and conferencing, revising, publishing—to respond to literature and to create characters, settings, and plots for their own stories. The product of the writing process is valuable because it's "assessable": How well does the student perform during each step? How well does the student recognize and/or employ these essential literary elements?

Though we tend to think of this linear approach as the way writers actually begin and carry out their story ideas, this is rarely the case. The linear approach is a sort of end-product in its own right. Before they get to these sequential steps, most writers have done a lot of nonlinear thinking: they have thought recursively.

2. The Recursive Approach

Recursive means "returning," going back and forth between one concept or element to another. For example, before setting pen to paper or finger to keyboard, the writer (student or professional) might have had an idea for setting, flashed back to a personal experience, tentatively thought of two characters, roughly sketched out a plot, revised the setting, made notes about a conflict, revised the characters to fit the conflict, then jotted down some significant dialogue recalled from the personal experience! In essence, the writer is revising before drafting, or envisioning a final product and then self-conferencing to redraft it, or going through some other recursive gyration to work out the story mentally before using the linear "writing process." That's the way most writers work.

Obviously, the recursive approach cannot be taught or assessed, because it is a highly individual process; people's minds "jump around" in idiosyncratic and uniquely imaginative ways. But the recursive approach can and should be encouraged because it provides the sparks and seeds that make students' responses to literature and students' own stories sparkle and develop.

Some of the activities in this book encourage the recursive thinking that feeds into writing about literature and into writing one's own stories. For example:

1. Free-Writes/Free-Reads
The writer is her or his best audience! By reading first thoughts or random drafts aloud to a partner or to a small group of classmates, the writer usually learns more about writing than through any other process. (The role of the audience here is to "just listen": no comments, positive or negative. The writer, if she or he wishes, can comment on the piece of writing.)

2. Variations on Read-Alongs
Voice is the message! Different readers interpret literature in different ways. By reading literary selections aloud in their own way, students begin to discover the selection's meaning for themselves.

3. Dialogues With Teacher and Classmates and Literature Circles
Ideas engender ideas! By freely sharing responses to a story, students uncover and develop insights into the personal significance of the story.

4. Visual Interpretations
One picture can capture the essence! By drawing story pictures and then studying what they've drawn, readers focus on the literary elements that impress them in a story.

5. Reading-Writing Journals
All your thoughts are important and can be useful to you as you write! Even snippets and brief notes should be treasured and filed. The merest notation might turn out to be the foundation of a great book report, or the key inspiration for a story.

TEACHER AND STUDENTS LEARNING TOGETHER
We think you'll agree: learning about literature and learning through literature are lifelong pursuits. Happily for avid readers, there's no end to the discoveries one can

make through reading great stories and through trying one's hand at writing them.

Most of the suggestions we've presented here are as relevant to adult literature buffs as they are to young people. Choose some of the activities to carry out on your own. Share the results with your students. Your enthusiasm for, curiosity about, and insights into wonderful stories are the most important factors in developing another generation of thoughtful and sensitive readers and writers.

ASSESSMENT TOOLS AND GUIDES

On pages 81–89, you'll find a variety of reproducible assessment pages and reading/writing guides that you and your students can use to track progress in understanding and using *Teaching Literary Elements*. We suggest that you preview the pages so that you can decide when to use them. Various sequences are possible. For example, students might use the Reader's Survey and the Readers-As-Writers Surveys on pages 81 and 85 before beginning the sequence of instruction in this book, and then again after they've completed it.

Character

When we as adults look back to and discuss books we've loved, it's usually the memorable characters in them that first come to mind: the selfish but courageous Scarlett O'Hara, for example, or the kind but "clueless" Emma Woodhouse. It's the compelling characters that quickly hooked us and kept us reading.

It's the same with young readers, of course. They, too, get glued to a story when the protagonist—the main character—reminds them strongly of themselves or of people they know or when the protagonist's hopes, needs, frailties, values, puzzlements, and problems/solutions echo the reader's view of her/himself. So, character is a natural, familiar literary element for students to consider as they begin to explore how literature works.

Here are the major thinking skills students will use and questions they'll address as they consider **character**:

CRITIQUE. What seems real and true to me about the characters in this story? How are the characters like those in other books I've read? How are they like me and people I know?

ANALYZE. What strategies does the author use that help me understand the characters and care about them?

SYNTHESIZE. How can I use what I've learned to develop the characters in my own stories?

Have on hand:

- If possible, multiple copies of two or three books that you feel do an especially good job of developing characters. See the Bibliography for suggestions.
- For each student: copies of the excerpts from *Call It Courage* (pages 22–23) and *The Talking Earth* (pages 24–25); and of Reader's Explorer 1 (page 27).

Build On Experience

Define the Literary Term

REVIEW   Explain to or review with students that a *character* is a person or an animal in a story, play, poem, or other work of literature. On the chalkboard, make a chart like the one that follows to organize students' identifications of characters they're already familiar with. Provide examples as start-ups.

A CHARACTER IN A...

Fairy Tale, Fable, Fantasy	Myth or Legend	Real-Life Story
Cinderella	Hercules	Julie, in *Julie of the Wolves*
The fox, in "The Fox and the Grapes"	Coyote, in "Coyote Steals the Moon"	Tom, in *Tom Sawyer*
Bilbo Boggins	Loki, the Trickster	Tituba, in *Tituba of Salem Village*

Brainstorm About Unforgettable Characters

MODEL AND PROMPT

Name and briefly describe a favorite character that pops into your mind, and tell why that character is so memorable to you. Example: "A character I'll never forget is Rufus Moffat. I guess I'll always remember Rufus because he's so determined! For example, he works so hard to get a library card!" Encourage students to name other story characters who have that attribute, e.g., determination: Winnie-the-Pooh, determined to get honey from the bee-tree; Adam, in *Adam of the Road*, determined to find his father; Sam, in *My Side of the Mountain*, determined to live alone in the wilderness.

BUILD A CHALKBOARD CHART

Ask students: "Who are some of your favorite story characters? Give us a word or phrase that describes the character. Let's think of other characters who fit that description." Encourage ESL students and/or students who haven't done much reading to contribute ideas from book spin-offs—for example, Ms. Frizzle from the Magic School Bus TV series or the movie characters Sarah from *A Little Princess* and James from *James and the Giant Peach*.

Your chalkboard brainstorm chart may look something like the one that follows. Use the chart to help students summarize their observations about why it is that we remember so clearly certain characters from stories. For example, they remind us of ourselves; they're like characters in other stories we've enjoyed; they have problems that are much like ours; we admire them; we worry about what will happen to them.

Character	Main Characteristic
Rufus Sam Adam the fox	Determined
Ms. Frizzle Winnie-the-Pooh Harriet (the Spy)	Great imagination!
Julie James Tituba Cinderella	Brave
Coyote Loki Tom Sawyer Pippi	Mischievous

Students choose one section of the class's brainstorm chart and discuss the different ways in which the characters exhibit the common characteristic, e.g., bravery. Then the group plans and acts out an interview show in which group members play the parts of the story characters as the host asks them how they exhibited this characteristic.

Students write a letter to a favorite story character, telling why they enjoyed reading about him or her. Students read their letters to a partner or small group.

Explore a Character

Read-Along

Distribute copies of the excerpt from *Call It Courage* (pages 22–23). Explain that the main character, or protagonist, is a fifteen-year-old boy named Mafatu and that the story takes place long ago in a part of the world unfamiliar to many readers. On a globe, point out the general setting: the islands of the South Pacific Ocean. Give a prompt. For example, "I wonder if we have anything in common with a boy who lived so long ago and so far away from most of us." Ask students to read along silently as you read aloud. In your reading, stress the words and phrases that evoke Mafatu's fear—for example, "terrible morning," "great hurricane," "the little boy gasped," "buried his head against his mother's cold neck."

Echo reading is a good way to get students of different reading abilities to share a piece of literature together. Here's how: You or a skilled student reader reads just a few sentences of the excerpt aloud. Another student who needs reading practice then repeats the passage.

Teacher-Student Dialogue

SHARE REACTIONS TO THE LITERATURE

Feel free to get the discussion rolling by giving your own reactions to the excerpt. Prompt, when necessary, with questions or comments that help students further develop their own ideas. Example:

Teacher: When I read about Mafatu, I think about how different my life is from his! But then I also think about how I'm like Mafatu in many ways. Do you have those feelings?

Student A: I'm not like Mafatu. I'm not afraid of the ocean! I love the ocean! It's a great place to play.

Student B: Yeah, but suppose something awful happened to you in the ocean once!

Student C: Like Mafatu. His mother drowned in the ocean.

Student D: And he was with her when that happened!

Student B: I might be scared of the ocean forever after that!

Student D: I think Mafatu's problem is that he associates the ocean with death.

Student A: Well, some fears may be hard to get over.

Teacher: That's true! I sure know what fear feels like! (Offer an example of some fear of your own—e.g., the dark, dogs, being alone, loud noises—and how it may have started. Encourage students to name a few fears of real-life people and how the fears may have begun. Respect privacy by letting kids talk about "other people's" fears, not necessarily identifying these fears as their own—although they well may be!)

Interpret Visually

Have partners make picture panels. The panels should show in sequence the events that happened to Mafatu and his mother. Each picture should show Mafatu's facial expressions and include dialogue balloons or thought balloons. Invite partners to show and read their panels to a larger group. The group can discuss (1) what's similar about their visual renditions of the story; (2) what's different about the panels and how the differences help them understand something more about Mafatu.

Students discuss these questions: What other books have we read in which the main characters are very much afraid? What are they afraid of, and why? Is it interesting to read about characters who are fearful? Why or why not? What do we hope will happen by the time the story ends?

Suggest that Circle members create a visual organizer as a way of sharing their ideas with classmates.

 Students can write Reflective Entries about major fears people have today. The journal writer can simply list different fears or concentrate on one fear and give examples or "why's." Suggest ways to file this journal page—for example, Story Ideas, or Ideas for Story Characters.

How a Character Is Developed

Your students can explore the five basic ways in which a writer reveals what a character is like.

DIRECT CHARACTERIZATION

1. The writer states directly what the character is like. Example: Rita was small and fragile looking, but she had immense courage and independence.

INDIRECT CHARACTERIZATION

2. The writer gives the actual speech of the character. Example: "I'm afraid but I'll do it anyway!" said Rita.

3. The writer reveals what the character is thinking or feeling. Example: As the cold water of the lake wrapped around her legs, Rita trembled at the memory of last summer's accident.

4. The writer tells about the character's actions. Example: With determined effort, Rita managed to get the rowboat into the lake and clamber aboard.

5. The writer tells how other people respond to the character. Example: Polly watched from the shore, knowing it was impossible to stop Rita once she had decided to do something. "She's so stubborn!" Polly thought.

Read-Along

Distribute copies of the excerpt from *The Talking Earth* (page 24–25). Explain that these are the first paragraphs of the book and that the main character is Billie Wind, a teenage girl who is a Seminole Indian. Tell students that the Seminoles' home base is in the Everglades of Florida. On a map of the United States, point out this geographical region. Provide a prompt. For example: "I'll read this aloud as you follow along. Let's listen for clues as to what Billie Wind is like."

VARIATION: STOP-GO READING

Stop-Go Reading is a good way to give several students an opportunity to read literature aloud. Here's how: One student reads aloud while classmates listen and follow along. At some point, the oral reader says "Stop-Go!" and calls on a classmate by name—for example, "Stop-Go! Albert." The second student picks up from there and then "Stop-Goes" for another classmate.

Read, Comment, Ask

Invite partners to reread and discuss the excerpt together and write questions and comments in the margins of their copies of the excerpt. Questions may be about unfamiliar terms, puzzling situations, or what happens next. Comments might include predictions, assessments of character, or notes about how the literature relates to the student's own life. As an example, you may wish to reproduce the following example on the chalkboard or as hand outs:

Billie Wind could see the orange tree through the open walls of the council house. A white bird floated down upon it, and she wondered if it had a nest nearby. "Billie Wind." The medicine man was speaking. "May I have your attention?" She was standing beside her sister Mary in the dim light of the house. Outside the sunlight was white and hot. Inside a soft trade wind blew under the palm-thatched roof, cooling the air pleasantly. Charlie Wind, the medicine man, who was also her uncle and friend, cleared his throat.

What's a council house?

Billie seems to be interested in nature.

What's a medicine man?

I guess Billie is not paying attention!

I'd like to know what a trade wind is.

Billie seems to be surrounded by family.

"Billie Wind," he repeated. "May I have your attention?" She promptly looked from the bird to the dark eyes of the elderly man.

I know what it's like to have adults demand your attention when you're thinking about something else!

"It is told that you do not believe in the animal gods who talk." He frowned.

Why does he frown? Maybe he's upset by Billie not sharing his belief. I don't believe in talking animal gods either!

Teacher-Student Dialogue

SHARE REACTIONS TO THE LITERATURE

Direct your prompts to help students focus on how Billie's character is revealed in the excerpt. Example:

Teacher: We've read just the very beginning of the book, but I already have some ideas about what Billie Wind is like. What do you think she's like?

Student A: I think she's interested in nature.

Teacher: What clues tell you that?

(Students may cite passages that indicate Billie's interest in birds.)

Teacher: How about Charlie Wind? Do you pick up some clues about what he's like?

Student B: He's very traditional. He wears old Seminole clothes.

Student C: And he has old Seminole beliefs, like animal gods that talk.

Student D: And he doesn't approve of Billie Wind.

Teacher: I wonder why that's so.

Student A: Well, she has a hard time paying attention to Charlie.

Student B: And she doesn't share his belief in animal gods.

Student C: She almost giggles when he talks about them.

Student D: And she doesn't take it seriously when Charlie says she has to be punished.

Teacher: It seems like you've found out a lot about characters just from these few paragraphs. Let's figure out what clues the writer provided.

Focusing On Five Methods

Copy the following chart on the chalkboard or make and distribute copies of it. Make sure students have their annotated copies of the excerpt from *The Talking Earth* to refer to. Work through the chart orally with the class, method by method, and invite students to find additional examples of each method. Be flexible: writers often combine methods, as in "'Yes,' she answered and smiled, tightening her lips so she would not giggle." (Character's words + Character's actions)

Invite the class to review the excerpt from *Call It Courage* to find examples of some of the methods. Examples:

❁ *It was the sea that Mafatu feared.* (The writer tells us directly what Mafatu is like.)

✣ *He felt that something was terribly wrong.* (The writer reveals what the character is feeling.)

✣ *He clung to his mother's neck.* (The writer tells about the character's actions.)

HOW WE KNOW ABOUT CHARACTERS

METHOD	EXAMPLE
1. The writer tells us directly.	She was standing beside her sister Mary in the dim light of the house.
2. The writer gives the actual words of the character.	"We believe that each person is part of a Great Spirit."
3. The writer reveals what a character is feeling or thinking.	She knew perfectly well these men did not believe in the serpent and the talking animals and the dwarfs.
4. The writer tells about characters' actions.	But they did not even smile. Charlie Wind crossed his arms on his chest.
5. The writer tells how other people respond to a character.	"...We are disturbed by your doubts."

Make Up a Character Together

Invite the class to make up a character and then compose examples of the five ways of revealing that character. The character might be a fable-like animal, a fairy-tale character, or a realistic person. Make a chalkboard web to incorporate students' ideas. Example:

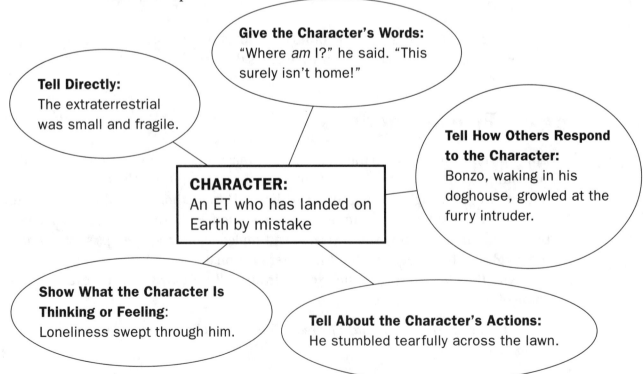

Give the Character's Words: "Where *am* I?" he said. "This surely isn't home!"

Tell Directly: The extraterrestrial was small and fragile.

CHARACTER: An ET who has landed on Earth by mistake

Tell How Others Respond to the Character: Bonzo, waking in his doghouse, growled at the furry intruder.

Show What the Character Is Thinking or Feeling: Loneliness swept through him.

Tell About the Character's Actions: He stumbled tearfully across the lawn.

Use the completed web to summarize and affirm what your student readers and writers have accomplished so far:

❈ They've read literature carefully and thoughtfully.

❈ They've found examples of different ways to reveal a character.

❈ They've used a writer's methods to begin to develop a fictional character of their own.

Eager writers may wish at this point to continue and flesh out the story the class began via the web. Encourage these writers to use the methods in the web. Through a free-read to a partner or small group, writers hear what they've written and make any changes or additions they wish.

Draw a "Character Outline"

ESL students and students who are primarily visual thinkers can use a visual like that on page 26 to concretize a character's feelings, thoughts, words, and actions. Partners may use a character the class has been studying (e.g., Mafatu or Billie Wind); a character from another book the partners are familiar with; or a new character, such as the one the class has begun to develop via the web on page 18. If necessary, provide examples. Suggest that partners show their finished outlines to a larger group or incorporate them into their Journals.

Suggest that Literature Circles share and discuss the annotations group members made as they read the selection from *The Talking Earth*. Students can help one another find answers to questions, identify areas of agreement and disagreement, and point out phrases and sentences that help them get to know Billie Wind. Two or more Literature Circles can then get together to discuss this question: How do commenting on and discussing this piece of literature help me to understand and enjoy it?

Challenge Activity: Use Reader's Explorer 1

This Reader's Explorer (page 27) provides a format for comparing and contrasting the main characters from two different books. The activity is designed for partners who've read both books. Ahead of time, prepare a list of character pairs for students to consider. Examples:

❀ Miyax in *Julie of the Wolves*; Sam in *My Side of the Mountain*

❀ Mafatu in *Call It Courage*; Karana in *Island of the Blue Dolphins*

❀ Sookan in *Echoes of the White Giraffe*; Yuki in *Journey Home*

Partners may, of course, choose other character pairs. See the Bibliography for ideas. (Note that this is an *open* compare-and-contrast: Students use brainstorming to identify as many differences and similarities as they can. After this broad consideration, students then zero in on the similarities and differences that are significant to the Focus Question that concludes the activity.)

Write About a Character

In this step, students will create a character of their own, following the writing process and applying the methods and insights they've developed so far. Prepare for the prewriting step by clipping from magazines and newspapers several photos (ideally, one for each student) of people in action or in unusual settings. The people portrayed should not be recognizable or well known to students. Aim for a collection that shows ordinary people with expressive faces and postures, engaged in situations that kids can relate to. Examples: an athlete straining to get over a hurdle; a young person cuddling a pet; a windblown pedestrian walking down a rainy street; a homeless person huddled in a doorway.

Prewriting

As you distribute the photos from your collection, explain to students that the pictures show ordinary people who can be turned into story characters. By using a writer's methods, students can make these characters interesting to readers. Model: Use one of the photos to demonstrate as you write on the chalkboard. Examples:

Appearance (What the Character Looks Like):
An old man with a scraggly beard and matted hair. Tattered coat. Eyes look sad. He's wearing floppy boots.

Actions (What the Character Is Doing):
Leaning on a doorway. Holding out his hand. Staring at something or someone.

Ask students to prewrite by making appearance and actions notes about the person shown in their photos.

Drafting

Ask students to use their prewriting notes to draft a paragraph about their character. In the draft, students can also imagine what the character is thinking, feeling, and hearing and how an observer reacts to the character. Model:

> The sad old man leans on the doorway. He clutches a ragged coat around him as the cold wind whistles and the sleet pelts down. He is remembering the warm fireplace in his childhood home. He would like to share that memory. But people pass by him with just a sideways glance. They are a little afraid of this aged man with his scraggly beard and his outstretched hand.

Revising

Have students work with a partner to revise their drafts. Write the following questions on the chalkboard or on poster paper to focus partners' observations and comments:

1. Did you tell me what the character looks like and what she or he does?

2. Did you let me know what the character is thinking and feeling?

3. Did you tell me how other people react to the character?

Partners can point out places in the draft where the writer might incorporate any of the elements above that are missing or that need clarification or expansion.

Ask students to make a clean copy of their character descriptions, using any comments and suggestions from their revision partner that they feel are on target and improve the description.

Teaching HINT Some students may want to work characters' exact words into their draft. Encourage this method, but consider your instructional options at this point. If your students know the mechanics of written dialogue (interior punctuation, capitals, paragraphing, etc.), urge them to use them. If you're about to teach or review these mechanics anyway, this may be a good place to stop for instruction; use the excerpt from *The Talking Earth* for examples. For some students, an insistence on mechanics might discourage their use of dialogue. Instead, present a broad-based concept—for example, put a character's actual words inside quotation marks.

Publishing

Display the photos on a bulletin board. Call on students randomly to read their descriptions aloud. Ask the audience to identify the photo the description refers to. What clues does the description provide? How does the description help us know more about the character and get us interested in the character?

Ask students to attach the pictures and descriptions and place them in a folder titled Possible Characters for Our Stories. Use the folder as a class writing resource.

From *Call It Courage*, by Armstrong Sperry

It was the sea that Mafatu feared. He had been surrounded by it ever since he was born. The thunder of it filled his ears; the crash of it upon the reef, the mutter of it at sunset, the threat and fury of its storms—on every hand, wherever he turned—the sea.

He could not remember when the fear of it first had taken hold of him. Perhaps it was during the great hurricane which swept Hikueru when he was a child of three. Even now, twelve years later, Mafatu could remember that terrible morning. His mother had taken him out to the barrier-reef to search for sea urchins in the reef pools. There were other canoes scattered at wide intervals along the reef. With late afternoon the other fishermen began to turn back. They shouted warnings to Mafatu's mother. It was the season of hurricane and the people of Hikueru were nervous and ill at ease, charged, it seemed, with an almost animal awareness of impending storm.

But when at last Mafatu's mother turned back toward shore, a swift current had set in around the shoulder of the reef-passage: a meeting of tides that swept like a millrace out into the open sea. It seized the frail craft in its swift race. Despite all the woman's skill, the canoe was carried on the crest of the churning tide, through the reef-passage, into the outer ocean.

Mafatu would never forget the sound of his mother's despairing cry. He didn't know then what it meant; but he felt that something was terribly wrong, and he set up a loud wailing. Night closed down upon them, swift as a frigate's wing, darkening the known world. The wind of the open ocean rushed in at them, screaming. Waves lifted and struck at one another, their crests hissing with spray. The poles of the outrigger were torn from their thwarts. The woman sprang forward to seize her child as the canoe capsized. The little boy gasped when the cold water struck him. He clung

to his mother's neck. Moana, the Sea God, was reaching up for them, seeking to draw them down to his dark heart. . . .

Off the tip of Hikueru, the uninhabited islet of Tekoto lay shrouded in darkness. It was scarcely more than a ledge of coral, almost awash. The swift current bore directly down upon the islet.

Dawn found the woman still clinging to the purau pole and the little boy with his arms locked about his mother's neck. The grim light revealed sharks circling, circling. . . . Little Mafatu buried his head against his mother's cold neck. He was filled with terror. He even forgot the thirst that burned his throat. But the palms of Tekoto beckoned with their promise of life, and the woman fought on.

When at last they were cast up on the pinnacle of coral, Mafatu's mother crawled ashore with scarcely enough strength left to pull her child beyond reach of the sea's hungry fingers. The little boy was too weak even to cry. At hand lay a cracked coconut; the woman managed to press the cool, sustaining meat to her child's lips before she died.

From *The Talking Earth*, by Jean Craighead George

Billie Wind could see the orange tree through the open walls of the council house. A white bird floated down upon it, and she wondered if it had a nest nearby.

"Billie Wind." The medicine man was speaking. "May I have your attention?" She was standing beside her sister Mary in the dim light of the house. Outside the sunlight was white and hot. Inside a soft trade wind blew under the palm-thatched roof, cooling the air pleasantly. Charlie

Wind, the medicine man, who was also her uncle and friend, cleared his throat.

"Billie Wind," he repeated. "May I have your attention?" She promptly looked from the bird to the dark eyes of the elderly man.

"It is told that you do not believe in the animal gods who talk." He frowned.

"It is told that you do not believe that there is a great serpent who lives in the Everglades and punishes bad Seminoles." He shook his head, then cast a sober glance at the councilmen, who were seated on the hard earth around him.

"And it is told that you doubt that there are little people who live underground and play tricks on our people." He pulled his white Seminole cape closer around his lean shoulders, forcing Billie Wind to notice that it was too long. It almost touched the black-and-white border of his skirt.

"Are you listening to me?"

"Yes," she answered and smiled, tightening her lips so she would not giggle.

"The council has met. We are disturbed by your doubts."

Billie Wind caught her breath. She knew perfectly well these men did not believe in the serpent and the talking animals and the dwarfs. They were educated and wise men. She knew them well. Several were her uncles, others were the fathers of her best friends. She waited for them to laugh understandingly as they usually did when the old legends and beliefs were discussed.

But they did not even smile. Charlie Wind crossed his arms on his chest.

"We are a tribe of the Seminole Indians," he said in a solemn voice. "We believe that each person is part of the Great Spirit who is the wind and the rain and the sun and the earth, and the air above the earth. Therefore we can not order or command anyone." He paused. "But we do agree that you should be punished for being a doubter."

Billie Wind glanced from face to face, searching for the good humor that would soon end this to-do about serpents and dwarfs. No one smiled, not even her comical uncle, Three-Hands-on-the-Saddle.

"What do you think would be a suitable punishment for you, Billie Wind?"

She let her mind wander, waiting for someone to break the silence and send her off to play. When it became apparent that this would not happen, she concentrated on a punishment: something ridiculous, something they would not let her do, it would be so dangerous.

"I think," she said with dignity, "that I should go into the pa-hay-okee, the Everglades, where these spirits dwell, and stay until I hear the animals talk, see the serpent and meet the little people who live underground."

"Good," he said, much to her surprise.

Name _____ Date _____

Character's Name: _____

Character's Thoughts and Feelings:

_____
_____
_____
_____
_____
_____
_____
_____

Character's Words:

_____
_____
_____
_____
_____

Character's Actions:

_____
_____
_____
_____
_____
_____

Reader's Explorer 1:
COMPARE AND CONTRAST

Name _____

Date _____

Character 1:

Name: _____

Book: _____

Character 2:

Name: _____

Book: _____

HOW ARE THE CHARACTERS ALIKE?

_____

_____

_____

HOW ARE THE CHARACTERS DIFFERENT?
With regard to:

_____	Where they	_____
_____	live	_____
_____		_____
_____	Their	_____
_____	personalities	_____
_____		_____
_____	Their main	_____
_____	problem	_____
_____		_____
_____	What they must	_____
_____	do to solve	_____
_____	the problem	_____

FOCUS QUESTION:

In your opinion: Which *likeness* between the characters is strongest?

_____

Which *difference* is strongest? _____

_____

Setting

Setting is the time and place in which story events happen. Settings are as crucial to what literary characters think and do as real-life environments are to our own thoughts and actions. As readers mature, we want them to assess the characters they read about in the context of the characters' surroundings.

Setting can be as dynamic and lively in its own way as characters are. On a simple level, for example, the weather in a place can change so radically over the course of a day that it forever affects a character's life, as it does Mafatu's in *Call It Courage*. On a more complex level, the customs and beliefs of a family or cultural group strongly influence a character's attitudes and actions, as they do Billie Wind's in *The Talking Earth*.

Exploring setting can be exciting and fruitful for students when they're engaged in activities that call upon their own sensory perceptions and their observations of people and situations in their own environments. Here are the major thinking skills students will use and questions they'll address as they consider setting:

OBSERVE. What's special about the setting in which *I* live?

ANALYZE. What strategies do writers use to make a setting clear to readers?

SYNTHESIZE AND APPLY. How can I use what I've learned to develop settings in my own stories?

Have on hand:

❈ Students' copies of the excerpts from *Call It Courage* (pages 22–23) and *The Talking Earth* (pages 24–25).

❈ If possible, multiple copies of two or three books that you feel do an especially good job of developing setting. See the Bibliography for suggestions.

❀ Several picture books that have evocative, exciting illustrations of story setting. (See the Bibliography.)

❀ For each student, a disposable camera.

❀ Copies of Reader's Explorer 2 (page 42).

Build On Experience

Define the Literary Term

REVIEW   Explain to or review with students that *setting* is the where-and-when of a story, the place and time in which a story character lives. On the chalkboard, make a web like the one that follows to organize students' recollections of places and times in which stories they're familiar with take place. (Examples are given.)

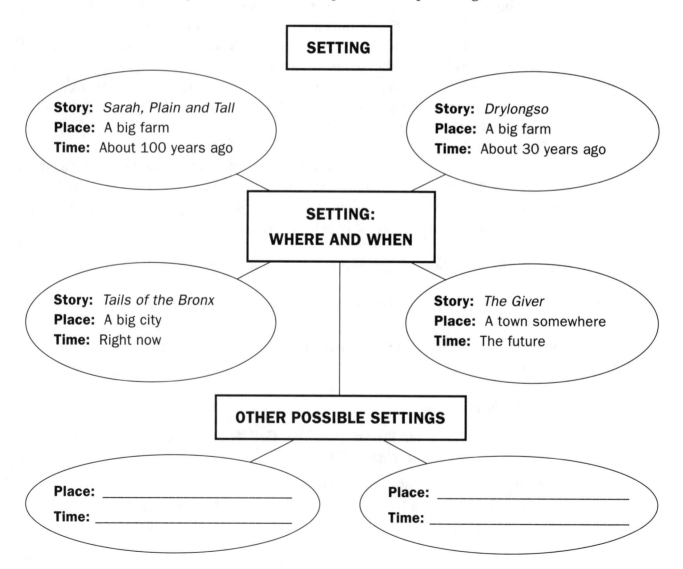

SETTING

Story: *Sarah, Plain and Tall*
Place: A big farm
Time: About 100 years ago

Story: *Drylongso*
Place: A big farm
Time: About 30 years ago

SETTING:
WHERE AND WHEN

Story: *Tails of the Bronx*
Place: A big city
Time: Right now

Story: *The Giver*
Place: A town somewhere
Time: The future

OTHER POSSIBLE SETTINGS

Place: _____
Time: _____

Place: _____
Time: _____

Next, ask students to imagine other possible settings for stories, perhaps for stories they themselves might write. Enter students' ideas, making additional circles as necessary. Students may suggest current, real-life settings (e.g., our town, today) or settings in distant places and/or other times (e.g., Egypt, three thousand years ago, a planet in the Spiral Galaxy, 200 years from now).

Conclude the activity by encouraging some preliminary ideas about how setting affects characters. Would a character in ancient Egypt have the same kind of life as a character on a distant planet many years from now? (Why/why not?)

 Students can write a Think-About-Your-Thoughts entry. This kind of journal page provides practice in the skill of metacognition: students have to consider *why* they made their choices. Create a chart like the one below on the chalkboard or on poster paper, with suggestions for a page format and headings. You may wish to provide examples.

If I Were a Character in a Story, Here's the SETTING I'd Use:

PLACE	WHY I CHOOSE THIS PLACE:
A distant planet	I like exploring and adventures. I think there would be a lot of challenges and excitement in a place very different from Earth.

TIME	WHY I CHOOSE THIS TIME:
About 20 years from now	By then, space travel to distant planets might really be possible. By then, I might have the skills to take part in interplanetary exploration.

Ask journal-keepers to file their charts under a label that will be helpful to them when they write, e.g., Exciting Story Settings.

Take Pictures of Real-Life Settings

For this step, each student will need a disposable camera. (See Have on Hand, pages 29–30.) By taking photographs of their own environment, and then talking and writing about the photos, students focus —in more ways than one!—on the details that make a time and place special and interesting. Here's the procedure:

PLAN AHEAD

The activity can be carried out in various ways. You may wish to make it a class Photography Field Trip, in which you and your students explore your community for a couple of hours. Other possibilities include: small-group expeditions in the school neighborhood, with parent volunteers monitoring the group; individual expeditions in which each student—perhaps accompanied by a parent or other at-home adult— carries out the assignment after school; a lunchtime or recess-time activity, in which students take pictures within the boundaries of your school and its grounds.

Arrange for the photos to be developed and delivered as quickly as possible (using one-hour or overnight development labs) so that you can build on the experience while it's still fresh in students' memories.

EXPLAIN THE TASK

Students will be roving photographers, taking pictures of places and scenes nearby that strike them as interesting. Suggest possible subjects: buildings and storefronts; fields; playgrounds; people at work or just walking along; friends and families outdoors or on porches and stoops; animals (e.g., birds, squirrels, dogs, cats). Also suggest to students that some of their photos might be close-ups, while others might show scenes from a distance. How about different angles? For example, can you take a picture of a person from a puppy's-eye view?

DISCUSS THE EXPERIENCE

Before their developed pictures arrive, students can briefly discuss what their cameras helped them "see." Why did they focus on particular scenes or objects? As they were aiming and focusing, what particular details were they hoping to capture on film? Does using a camera help them notice things more carefully than they usually do without a camera? If so, why?

Choose Your Best Photos

After you've given each student his or her developed photos, ask the student to select the three or four that he or she likes best. Then have students discuss with a partner why they especially like these pictures. If you've participated in this step by snapping your own photos, you can model. Examples: "I like this up-close photo because it shows all the cracks in the steps up to the house and the grass and other plants growing out of the cracks. I don't think I ever noticed these before." "I like this photo because it shows a lot of different things from a distance. There's my neighbor watering his plants. There's Snowflake, Mrs. Murphy's cat, sitting in the window. There's my garage: Wow, I never realized until now how much it needs painting!"

Ask each student to label each of his or her favorite photos with a where-and-when caption and put them in their Journals to use again soon. See samples on the next page.

Explore Setting

Read-Along

Your students have probably already studied the excerpt from *Call It Courage* (pages 22–23) in their investigation of character. Now's the time to return to this excerpt to

explore setting. Ask students to read their copies of the excerpt silently as you read aloud and to underline the phrases and sentences that help them see the *place* in their mind's eye. In your reading, you may wish to stress the phrases that evoke setting, e.g., "...the thunder of it"; "...canoes scattered at wide intervals along the reef"; "...their crests hissing spray"; "...shrouded in darkness"; "The grim light revealed sharks circling, circling...."; "...the sea's hungry fingers."

VARIATION: PARTNER THINK-ALOUD

A Partner Think-Aloud allows pairs of students to get immediate feedback as they read a piece of literature together. Here's how: A partner reads aloud some sentences of the selection, stopping at a point where he or she is impressed by a particular image or idea. The reader shares and discusses this reaction with the partner. Then the partner picks up the oral reading, stops, and discusses.

Teacher-Student Dialogue

SHARE REACTIONS TO THE LITERATURE

As a discussion participant, use questions, examples, and other prompts that help students focus on words, phrases, and comparisons that help readers envision the setting. Example:

Teacher: What's the general picture you get of the sea as you read this excerpt? Is it a calm place or a threatening one?

Student A: I think it's a scary place.

Teacher: I agree! In the very first paragraph, the words "thunder" and "crash" made me feel that this sea is rough and wild. Let's find more parts of this excerpt that build a scary setting.

[Students may cite words or phrases emphasized in the Read-Along (see above); other examples are "mutter," "threat and fury," "impending storm," "swift current," "churning tide," "darkening," "screaming," "hissing." Write students' choices on poster paper.]

Teacher: There are places in this excerpt where the setting—the sea—seems almost like a person. In fact, there's one place where the sea *is* a person. Can you find it in the fourth paragraph?

Student B: It's Moana, the Sea God.

Teacher: What's Moana doing?

Student C: Reaching up for them. Trying to draw them down.

Teacher: And there are words like" mutter" and "hissing" that are sounds that humans make. What are some other places in this excerpt where the sea acts like a human being?

Student D: Well, in the fourth paragraph the sea screams.

Student A: And right after that the waves strike each other, like people having a fight.

Teacher: Why do you think the writer used all these scary words and phrases?

Student B: He wants us to see a stormy ocean.

Student C: He wants us to see why Mafatu is afraid of the sea.

Student D: Yeah, but the ocean isn't always rough and scary.

Teacher: You're right. I remember playing in the ocean and feeling very safe and happy. But that was a different setting—a different time and place.

Interpret Visually

Some students might enjoy painting a seascape showing the ocean as described in the excerpt from *Call It Courage*. Display the paintings. Invite the artists to tell classmates what aspects of the setting they've incorporated into their work.

Investigate the Geography

Partners can use the definitions, explanations, and illustrations in dictionaries, encyclopedias, and world atlases to explore the terms *barrier reef, coral, current, island,* and *open ocean*. These terms—along with other words and phrases partners may choose from the excerpt—can then be used as labels in a schematic drawing that helps classmates understand the setting and what happens there.

 Circle members reread the first two paragraphs of the excerpt from *The Talking Earth* (pages 24–25) to find words and phrases that establish the setting. Examples: "...orange tree through the open walls of the council house," "dim light," "soft trade wind," "cooling the air pleasantly." Students can then discuss (1) the feelings this setting generates in readers (e.g., peaceful, happy, calm); (2) how Billie Wind feels in this setting (e.g., comfortable, at home); (3) how Billie Wind's feelings contrast with Mafatu's; and (4) how setting affects a character's feelings and actions.

Compose a "Found Poem"

A "found poem" is one that uses significant words and phrases from an existing piece of writing. In this case, students use words and phrases from the excerpt from *Call It Courage*. Ask students to look back at the words and phrases they underlined during the Read-Along (page 32) and share these orally. Line by line, write suggestions on the chalkboard:

> "The thunder of it..."
> " ...the crash of it upon the reef,"
> "...the mutter of it..."
> [and so on, through the excerpt]

You or a fluent student reader can then read the "found poem" aloud. Discuss how the found poem focuses on the nitty-gritty of setting. Some students may enjoy reworking and shortening the found poem to make it even more intense. Example:

> Thunder, crash, mutter,
> Threatened fury of the storm.
> Terrible morning.
> Tides like a millrace out to the sea.
> A darkening world, screaming.
> Grim light.
> Sharks circling, circling.

Your students may wish to copy the found poem in their Journals or use lines from it as captions for the paintings they and their classmates made (*Interpret Visually*, page 35).

How a Setting Is Developed

In good literature, settings are made real to us through the writer's use of precise words and phrases that appeal to our senses. The following activities can help students identify and appreciate how these word pictures are built and to construct word pictures of settings in their own writing.

A Visual Trip

You'll need: (1) a photo you yourself made during Step 2 or a favorite photo a student made and then labeled (page 32); (2) for each student, drawing paper and crayons, colored markers, or pencils. Your task is to describe the picture in enough detail (where, what, when, comparisons) so that students can draw a fairly accurate rendition of it without even seeing the photo.

PROCEDURE:

Ask students to close their eyes while you describe the setting. Tell students to listen carefully and envision the setting in their mind's eye so that they can draw a picture of it afterward. Example:

It's an old, empty building, four stories high, on a city street. Winter winds sweep around it and whistle through its cracked and broken windows. Its big door, once so strong, now rattles and creaks on its broken hinges. Inside, there's a musty smell. Once, many years ago, families lived in the building, and it was filled with laughter and talk. Now the building is just a shell. All around it are other buildings with lights shining out of the windows, humming with the sounds of people. On this frosty night, the old building seems as dark and gloomy as a mournful, sad ghost.

Students may want to hear a "return trip" before or as they draw. Display the finished art. On an overhead projector or on the chalkboard, show the verbal description above and invite a student to read it aloud. Ask the class to identify the words and phrases that appeal to the senses and that compare the old building to other things. Underline these words and phrases. Point out how these details enable students to see the setting in their mind's eye and actually re-create it in a picture.

Develop Your Photos With Words

This activity provides students with an immediate insight into the personal, affective meaning a chosen setting has for them. Ask students to retrieve their own favorite labeled photos (see pages 32–33) and exchange them with a partner. The partner chooses one of the photos, refers to the label, and writes a brief description (one or two sentences) of the setting. This description is likely to be pretty literal and cut-and-dried. Example:

It's a rainy Saturday. Someone is jumping up and down in a mud puddle.

Partners then discuss the descriptions. The student who made the photo tells

Dialogue:	Notes:
Student: It wasn't just rainy. It was a warm rain, like spring was already here.	warm, like spring
Partner: But it's not spring yet!	
S: That's what was so special. Just the day before, that puddle was solid ice!	ice yesterday water today
P: Oh, so the day before it was snow coming down, not rain.	
S: I think it was sleet. All the roads and sidewalks were slippery. Then overnight it all melted.	sleet, slippery melted
P: So who's this jumping in the puddle?	
S: I don't know. Just some little kid. He looked real happy.	a happy child
P: I like the way your picture shows all the splashes.	splash
S: I like that, too. It makes me remember that kind of whooshing sound that big boots make in a puddle.	a whooshing sound

about details she or he remembers from its setting. The partner questions, comments, and jots notes.

Partners give one another the notes they've made during the dialogues. Each student can use these notes soon to build a written description of the setting in the photo.

VARIATION: TEACHER MODEL/TAPE TALK

Modeling the dialogue provides a way to show students ahead of time how their partner dialogues might proceed. A tape of the dialogue can help a reluctant writer. How-To: Call on the "reluctant" writer to model with you while a small group of students listens and observes. Follow the procedure above, with you playing the part of the partner and making written notes. Tape the dialogue. Afterward, play the tape with your student partner and point out that the written notes you've made are based on the student's good ideas. Give the notes to the student to use as a word bank.

 Encourage students to free-write about the settings in their photos, using their partner's notes and other insights from the discussion. Students can read their descriptions to you or to the partner. Remind students of the parameters of a free-write/free-read: the "audience" is just the writer and another listener or two; the writer listens for and makes notes about what he or she likes and about what she or he would like to change; the "other listeners" just listen.

Three Explorations Into Setting

1. SETTING x TWO

On the chalkboard, draw a web with a quite "general" place (WHERE) at its center. (See the following example.) Ask students to imagine this place at a particular time

SEE
people swimming
whitecaps on the water
boats anchored offshore
kids' sandcastles
sandpipers running

HEAR
waves breaking
people laughing and talking
seagulls crying
a lifeguard's whistle
a breeze blowing

WHERE: THE SEASHORE
WHEN: A WARM, SUNNY DAY

TOUCH
the warmth of the sun
gritty sand
cool water
a seashell
a seagull feather

SMELL/TASTE
the smell of salt water
the taste of salt water
a big sandwich for lunch
sunscreen lotion
fish

(WHEN) and to suggest words and phrases that describe what they might see, hear, touch, smell, and taste at that place and time. Write suggestions in the appropriate boxes. Examples are given (see previous page).

Next, ask the class to imagine the same WHERE at a different time (WHEN). For example, the seashore on a stormy evening in autumn. Write the new WHEN. Ask: What items on our web don't belong there now? (Erase them, e.g., "the warmth of the sun.") What words and phrases can we write in their place? (e.g., "a cold wind")

Help the class summarize what they've learned through this activity: A *setting* is a place, plus all the things that we *sense* in that place. Ask students to suggest some ways this applies to settings they're familiar with—for example, your school at nine o'clock in the morning and at four in the afternoon, the playground on a summer evening and on a winter evening, a residential street at noon and at midnight.

2. CONTRAST AND COMPARE SETTINGS

Have students work with a partner. Randomly distribute to each pair slips of paper on which you've written general Wheres or Places—for example, a forest, an old house in the country, a city street, a mountaintop, a lake, a vacant lot, a gas station, a big store, a highway, a hospital. Each partner lists sensory words and phrases that come to mind when she or he sees this place in the mind's eye. Partners compare their lists and make a chart like the one that follows. Then partners discuss with another partner team: Where do our ideas for settings come from? (personal observations, feelings, experiences) How does a writer make sure readers "see" the setting the way she/he sees it? (use details; appeal to senses)

SETTING: A PLAYGROUND

	PARTNER 1 Name_____	PARTNER 2 Name_____
TIME:	After school, in the spring	Late at night in the winter
I SEE:	Kids shooting baskets	Snow on the swings
	My sister and her friend on the swings	A stray dog looking for food
I HEAR:	Kids shouting Traffic noises	The sound of sleet A siren
I FEEL:	Drops of perspiration A now-and-then breeze	A chilly wind Sleet on my face
I TASTE/SMELL:	Hamburgers cooking Traffic fumes	The coldness of snow A woodstove somewhere

On the basis of their charts and follow-up discussions, students might paint two-panel pictures of the contrasting settings or write two-stanza poems about the contrast.

3. EXPLORE PICTURE BOOK SETTINGS

Have on hand grade-level books that include fine illustrations. See the Bibliography for suggestions. (As an example, we are using here Thomas Locker's *Where the River Begins*.)

Have students work in groups of four or five. The group chooses a book, then selects an illustration within it that shows a setting that interests them. A group scribe can note <u>why</u> group members like the setting shown in the picture and any observations and questions they may have about it. Example:

Why We Like This Picture

I like the big gray and white clouds. Is a storm coming?

I like the sunshine lighting up the fields and the sheep.

People holding hands. Where are they going?

The water looks calm and peaceful.

It looks like warm weather. The people have summer clothes on.

Who lives in that little white house far away?

They started out <u>early</u> the next <u>morning</u>. For a time they walked along a <u>familiar road</u> past <u>fields of golden wheat</u> and <u>sheep grazing in the sun</u>. <u>Nearby</u> flowed the <u>river</u>—<u>gentle</u>, <u>wide</u>, and <u>deep</u>.

A group reader reads aloud the text that goes with the illustration. Group members listen for words and phrases that tell about the setting. (These are underlined in the excerpt.)

Next, the group discusses: What do the writer's words tell me that the picture *doesn't* tell me? Examples: the time of day, what the road is like to the people walking along it, what's growing in the fields, what the sheep are doing, that the water is a river, that the little house is probably where they started out from.

Finally, suggest that two or three groups come together to share illustrations, read the authors' words, and discuss how the words add to the illustration. Some students may enjoy writing their own paragraphs about the settings, using their group's notes.

 Circle members review a chapter book or novel they've enjoyed that has few or no illustrations. Students find passages that vividly describe setting, and identify words and phrases that appeal to specific senses. A Circle scribe can record these words. Encourage Circles to find a way of demonstrating the importance of the verbal descriptions. Example: (1) Read the passage, leaving out some of the description. (2) Rework the passage, changing the descriptions to change the setting—for example, a "gloomy" forest might become a "sunlit" forest, a street "bustling with traffic" might become a "silent street." (3) Draw an illustration to accompany the verbal description; discuss the phrases that helped artists make this words-to-picture translation.

Challenge Activity: Use Reader's Explorer 2

This Reader's Explorer (page 42) provides a format for developing *metaphors* as a way of describing settings. Students can carry out the exploration independently or with a partner. You may wish to prepare students for the activity by reviewing what a metaphor is: a figure of speech that compares one thing to another thing; some metaphors use *like* or *as*, and some don't. Present examples on the chalkboard:

❋ "The fog comes/ *on little cat feet...*"

❋ "Wind is *a cat that prowls at night...*"

❋ The fog comes in silently, *as a cat does.*

❋ Wind is *like a cat prowling at night.*

You may also wish to:

❋ Preview with students the Explorer headings and prompts. Suggest or brainstorm possible subjects for metaphors—for example, a lone tree in a park, an old abandoned building, a thunder cloud, an empty swing swaying back and forth in the wind, a full moon, a fire or police siren, rain (snow, sleet), a river or other body of water, a paper cup in a gutter, autumn leaves.

Reader's Explorer 2:
CREATE A METAPHOR

Name _____

Date _____

Here's What I Want to Describe: **What This Thing Is Like:**

_____   _____

_____   _____

DETAILS   **WHAT I WANT TO SAY:**   DETAILS

_____ **Characteristic:** _____

_____ Visual _____

_____ Appearance _____

_____ **Characteristic:** _____

_____ Sounds _____

_____ It Makes _____

_____ **Characteristic:** _____

_____ What It Feels Like _____

_____ if You Touch It _____

PUTTING IT ALL TOGETHER: Look at your work above. What are the main characteristics you'd like to emphasize? Underline them.

STATE YOUR METAPHOR: Use one or both of the sentence frames below.

The_____ is *like* a

_____

_____

The_____ is a

_____

_____

SHARE YOUR METAPHOR: Read it aloud to a partner. What do you think of your metaphor? If you wish, add to it or reword it.

Write About a Setting

In this step, students will create a story setting, following the writing process and applying the methods and insights they've developed so far.

Explain the assignment: students will write a paragraph that describes a place. The description should include several details and word pictures that appeal to the senses.

Prewriting

Ask students to pull together and review the rich store of setting ideas they've accumulated. Examples:

❀ Journal entries

❀ Photos, photo labels, and word lists based on partner discussions

❀ Free-writes

❀ Discoveries in Literature Circles

❀ Settings in picture books and in books without pictures

❀ Their own artwork that shows settings

❀ Completed Reader's Explorer 2

❀ (If your students have carried out the Write About a Character activity, page 20) A brief overview of a character in a setting

The student then decides what setting to develop and organizes details about it. You might suggest a Setting Wheel as a visual organizer and provide an example.

Drafting

Ask students to use their prewriting notes or a graphic organizer as they draft their paragraphs. Suggest that the first sentence in the paragraph identify the place for readers. Examples:

❀ The abandoned factory sits all alone on a huge lot.

❀ I've always felt sorry for the old, deserted building on 10th Avenue.

❀ Is a deserted building scary, or sad, or a little of both?

❀ People used to make shoes in this old building, but now the place is empty and abandoned, like a nest from which young birds have flown.

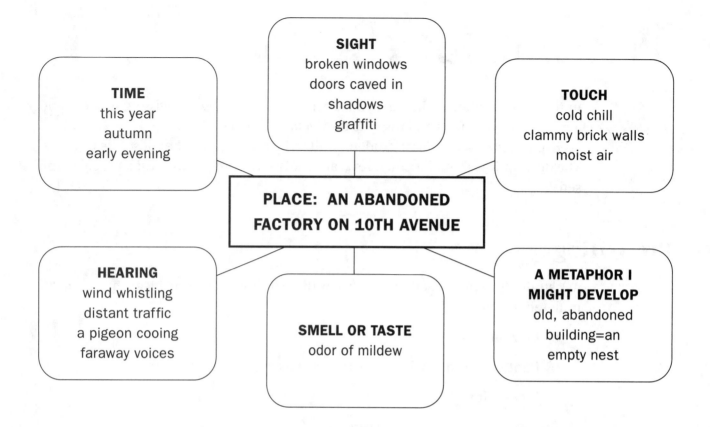

Explain that the opening sentence is like a kick-off point, to which the writer adds details to build the description of the setting.

Revising

Have students work with a partner to revise their drafts. Write the following questions on the chalkboard or on poster paper to focus partners' observations and comments.

1. Does the first sentence identify the place?

2. Does the rest of the paragraph use details that appeal to two or more senses?

3. Does the writer use comparisons or metaphors? If not, is there a place in the paragraph where a metaphor might be helpful?

Partners can point out places in the draft where the writer might incorporate any of the elements above that are missing or that need clarification or expansion. Remind students that reading aloud is a good way to assess a piece of writing: partners can read aloud as they try out revisions and test them against the original.

 As they revise their descriptions of setting, many students will be looking for precise words. This is an opportunity to review two writer's tools—the dictionary and the thesaurus. Show students how to use classroom dictionaries and junior thesauruses to find exact verbs, adjectives, and adverbs and replace overused words.

You might make a list that presents overused words and some possible alternatives; then ask students to find definitions of the latter and to suggest contexts in which they would be appropriate. Examples:

Overused Word	Alternatives	Example
BIG	tremendous	a *tremendous* dinosaur
	wide	a *wide* lake
	important	an *important* idea
BEAUTIFUL	handsome	a *handsome* building
	lovely	a *lovely* brook
	exquisite	an *exquisite* spider web
STRANGE	mysterious	a *mysterious* building
	unusual	an *unusual* sound
	odd	an *odd* sight

Publishing

After students have made a clean copy of their description of setting, suggest some publishing options:

❋ **Pair words and pictures.** Students can design a pair of pages, as in a book, in which a photo or illustration accompanies the written description. Paired pages can be incorporated into a Picture Book Possibilities folder.

❋ **Read your description aloud for a tape.** Students can contribute their tapes to the Writing Resource Center so that classmates can listen as they ponder various story ideas.

❋ **Get fast feedback from classmates.** Students can read their descriptions aloud to a small group of classmates, then ask the audience to brainstorm about events that might happen in that setting. Suggest that the writer take notes: this can be a powerful impetus for developing a plot.

❋ **Combine your setting description with your description of a character.** This is a Challenge activity for students who've completed a description of a character (page 20). Allow a lot of latitude. Some students may wish to write separate paragraphs—one about the character, one about the setting. Other students may choose to select details from both descriptions and present them together. Students can read aloud what they've written to a group of classmates.

Plot

*P*lot is the series of related events that happen in a story. As readers, we expect a plot to unfold in a clear way:

1. The *opening* lets us know who the characters are.

2. A *conflict* is presented. We find out what problem the main character or characters are facing.

3. Some *complications* arise as the character tries to resolve the conflict.

4. There's a *climax*—usually an event—in which the character has to choose a way to settle the conflict. The climax is usually the most exciting event in the story.

5. There's a *resolution*. The problem is solved and the story ends.

Cut-and-dried and traditional as these steps may be, and as much as we take them for granted as readers, plot is usually the most difficult literary element for writers—novice or experienced—to tackle. Writers may start off eloquently with characters and conflict, and even move realistically into complications. The bog-down points are usually climax and resolution. Many writers simply throw in the towel at this point. (How many of us, as teachers, have been disappointed with our students' "But-it-was-all-just-a-dream" conclusions to stories that were galloping along up until this point?)

To explore literary plots and to begin to take the necessary steps to incorporate plot into their own writing, students can use the following thinking skills to address these questions:

ANALYZE. What is the conflict the main character has to deal with?

PREDICT. What are some different ways the character might settle the conflict?

EVALUATE. What settlement of the conflict makes the most sense?

APPLY. What event or events make the character arrive at this settlement?

Have on Hand:

- Students' copies of the excerpts from *Call It Courage* (pages 22–23) and *The Talking Earth* (pages 24–25).
- If possible, multiple copies of two or three books that you feel have especially exciting and intriguing plots. See the Bibliography for suggestions.
- Copies of Reader's Explorer 3 (page 65).

Build On Experience

Define the Literary Term

REVIEW Explain to or review with students that a story plot is made up of the main things that happen in a story. Because folktales, fairy tales, and fables have simple plots, use one that's familiar to students as a chalkboard example. A plot stair is a useful visual because you can put the climax on the highest step. Examples:

STORY: The Fox and the Grapes

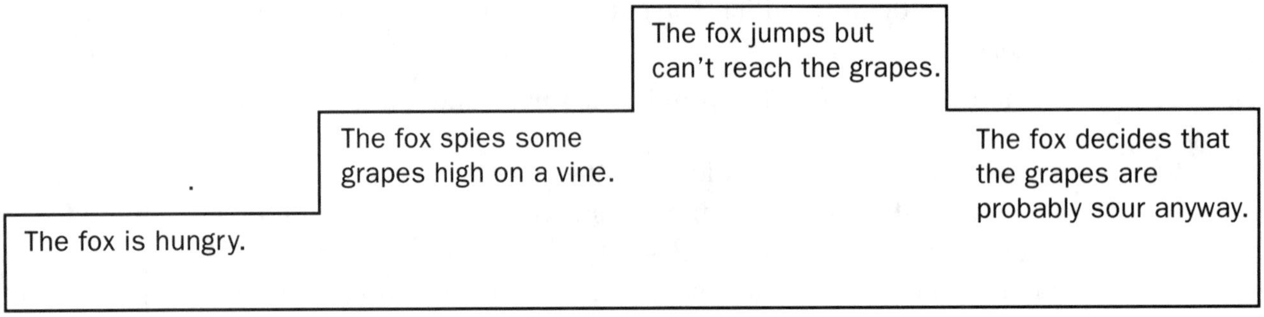
The fox is hungry.
The fox spies some grapes high on a vine.
The fox jumps but can't reach the grapes.
The fox decides that the grapes are probably sour anyway.

STORY: Beauty and the Beast

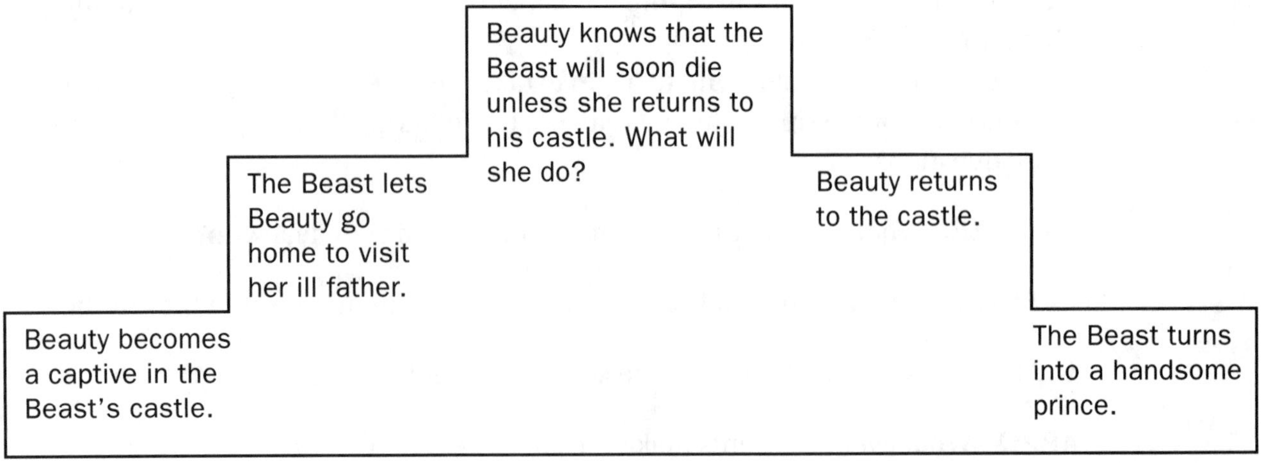
Beauty becomes a captive in the Beast's castle.
The Beast lets Beauty go home to visit her ill father.
Beauty knows that the Beast will soon die unless she returns to his castle. What will she do?
Beauty returns to the castle.
The Beast turns into a handsome prince.

Next, provide an activity that involves putting five events from a familiar story in sequence. Write the events on the chalkboard in random order. Draw an empty five-step plot stair, like the one in the Beauty and the Beast example. As students identify the sequence, write the steps or their numerals on the plot stair. Example, from the tale "Rumplestiltskin" (numerals in parentheses indicate the correct order):

The strange little man comes to the castle and claims the baby. **(2)**

One messenger discovers the little man's name. It's Rumplestiltskin. **(4)**

A miller's daughter promises to give her first child to a strange little man if he'll help her spin straw into gold. **(1)**

The girl tells the little man his name, and he stomps away furiously forever. **(5)**

The girl can only save her baby by guessing the little man's name. Can she do it? *How* can she do it? She sends messengers out throughout the kingdom. **(3)**

Ask a student to read aloud the class's plot steps in sequence. Affirm what students have accomplished:

❀ They've put plot steps in time order.

❀ They've identified sentence (3) as the high point of the story—the part of the story where the main character (the girl) must decide on a way to solve her Big Problem (how to keep her baby).

 Encourage students to free-write, using the final event on one of the plot stairs to imagine what might happen in the story *after* that. Students can write a paragraph about the new adventure or enter it on a plot stair of their own. As students read their paragraphs or explain their plot stairs to a partner, they can note any changes they'd like to make. Suggest that students put their free-writes into the Story Ideas sections of their Journals.

Explore a Plot

Read-Aloud

To begin developing insights into plot, it's usually most efficient to use a short story that you can read aloud in a single sitting. Some short story anthologies are suggested in the Bibliography.

Before you read, build student interest in the story through two or three clue-questions and hints. For example, if the story is Ray Bradbury's "All Summer in a Day":

❀ A lot of sci-fi is about humans from Earth who go to live on another planet, say the planet Venus. What do you think life on Venus might be like (weather, plants, survival techniques, work)?

- If you went to live on Venus, what do you think you'd miss most about Earth? Why?
- Imagine a school on Venus—for example, an elementary school in which the students are the children of pioneers from Earth. How might the students be the same as students here? How might they be different?

VARIATION: DIRECTED LISTENING/THINKING

Directed listening encourages students to listen for textual clues and to use prior knowledge to predict what will happen next in the story. This strategy provides a way for students to monitor their own comprehension: listening to the next part of the story, they verify or reject their predictions, then continue the cycle. Here's how: Ahead of time, note three or four "pause points"—places where there is more than one possibility of what the next event might be. Ask students to briefly list some things that might happen next. Then continue reading to the next pause point.

Teacher-Student Dialogue

SHARE REACTIONS TO THE LITERATURE

As a discussion participant and leader, your main role here is to help students focus on the major *events* in the story you've just shared with them. Two discussion guidelines:

1. Encourage students to focus on plot by building on concepts about characters and setting. For example, in dialoguing about "All Summer in a Day," you might ask: (Character) How is Margot different from her classmates? How do her classmates *treat* her? Why? What do they finally *do* to Margot that shows how they feel about her? How does Margot *react* to what her classmates do? (Setting) What is the weather on Venus like? What is going to *happen* to the weather? How do the children *act* as they anticipate this change? Why does Margot *stare* so hard out the classroom window? How do her classmates *behave* when the sun appears?
2. Encourage students to identify events in the story that filled them with feelings such as suspense, worry, excitement, anger, or curiosity. Record students ideas, using "when" sentence frames. Examples:
   - I was angry *when* William shoved Margot and made fun of her.
   - I was worried about Margot *when* she acted so silent and sad.
   - I felt suspense *when* the kids were waiting for the sun to appear.

Conclude by affirming what students have accomplished through the dialogue: They've focused on plot, the sequence of important events in the story.

Interpret Visually

In investigating character, your students may have made a rather freewheeling picture panel showing Mafatu (from *Call It Courage*) as he's caught in the hurricane (page 14). Here's an opportunity to help students—individually or with a partner—to use a picture panel to focus more closely on the aspects of plot, using the short story you've shared with them. The picture panel on page 52 is based on Ray Bradbury's "All Summer In a Day."

 In their Journals, students can draw a plot stair of five or six steps, filling in only, for now, the top step, which they can title "The Most Exciting Thing That Ever Happened to Me." Provide a format like that in the following example. Suggest that students fill in the other steps as ideas occur to them.

Suggest that students make a "Possible Plots" label for their Journals and file this plot stair under it.

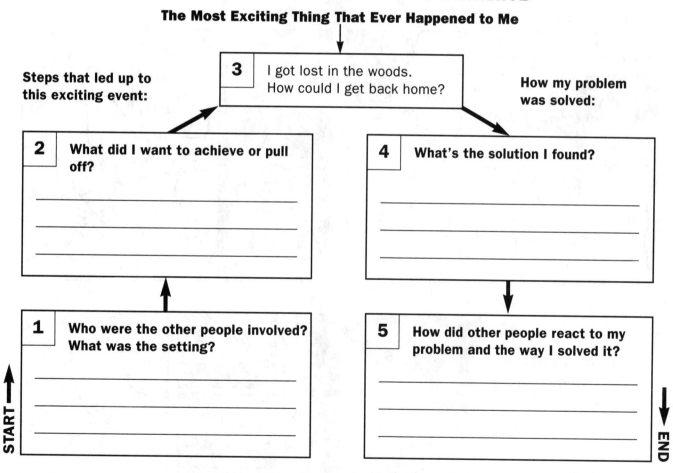

A PLOT BASED ON A PERSONAL EXPERIENCE
The Most Exciting Thing That Ever Happened to Me

Steps that led up to this exciting event:

3 I got lost in the woods. How could I get back home?

How my problem was solved:

2 What did I want to achieve or pull off?

4 What's the solution I found?

1 Who were the other people involved? What was the setting?

5 How did other people react to my problem and the way I solved it?

START

END

Here's something I learned from the experience:

Suggest that students make a "Possible Plots" label for their Journals and file this plot stair under it.

1. (OPENING) Who are the characters? What are they thinking as the story begins?

I miss Earth. I miss the sun.

The sun is going to come! What's the sun like?

2. (CONFLICT) What's the main problem between the characters?

These kids don't like me. They treat me like an outsider.

You're such a know-it-all! You're different! You live on Earth!

3. (COMPLICATION:) How do the characters try to settle the conflict?

4. (CLIMAX) What eventually settles the conflict?

Here's what the sun is like. Let me tell you what to expect.

Who'd believe Margot? She's such a nerd!

I can't believe this! These awful kids locked me up. Now I'll miss the sun!

Whoopee! Sun! How warm! Margot was absolutely right!

5. (RESOLUTION) How does the story end?

We're sorry, Margot! We forgot about you in the closet. We're sorry we were mean to you. The sun was so beautiful! You were right about how the sun looks and feels.

52

In most short stories, there is usually *one* critical or climactic event. In longer literature, there may be *many* critical events that make readers wonder "What will happen next?"

In chapter books, the writer usually ends a chapter at a high point where readers will ask this "What Next" question, thus urging them to read on to find the answer. Ask Literature Circles to choose a chapter book that all group members have read, (e.g., *The Talking Earth* or *Call It Courage*) and to discuss the event with which each chapter ends, then talk about what they expect the next chapter to reveal. Are the readers' expectations answered? Are there more surprises in store? When is it a good idea to divide a story into chapters?

How a Plot Is Developed

The "energy source" for most plots is a *conflict* between the main character (the *protagonist*) and another opposing force. The opposing force (the *antagonist*) can be another person, a natural phenomenon, pressure or resistance from a group, or some conflicting ideas in the main character's mind. Examples:

❀ In *The Wizard of Oz*, the main character, Dorothy, is opposed by a *person*: the "bad witch."

❀ In *Call It Courage*, the main character, Mafatu, is opposed by a *natural phenomenon*: the sea.

❀ In "All Summer in a Day," the main character, Margot, is opposed by a *group*: her classmates.

❀ In *The Talking Earth*, the main character, Billie Wind, must struggle with her own *conflicting ideas* about traditional beliefs and modern reality.

The following activities can help students identify story conflicts and see how a story plot must eventually resolve the conflict in a logical way.

Review and Build

Create a graphic organizer like the one that follows on a transparency or on the chalkboard. Students can use it to show the major conflicts in familiar stories and to review character and setting. Examples are shown in parentheses.

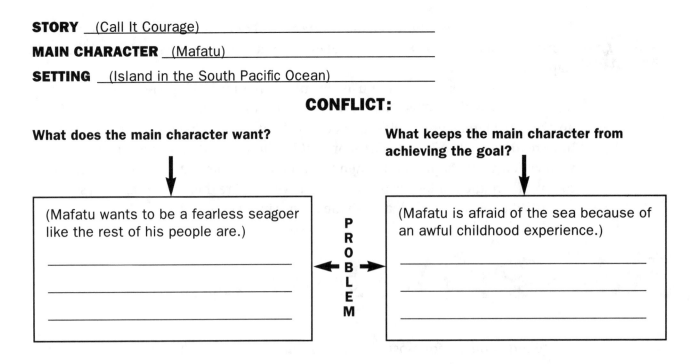

STORY _(Call It Courage)_

MAIN CHARACTER _(Mafatu)_

SETTING _(Island in the South Pacific Ocean)_

CONFLICT:

What does the main character want?

(Mafatu wants to be a fearless seagoer like the rest of his people are.)

_____

_____

_____

P R O B L E M

What keeps the main character from achieving the goal?

(Mafatu is afraid of the sea because of an awful childhood experience.)

_____

_____

_____

As students use the visual to tell about conflicts in other stories, help them to keep their summaries focused on the *main* conflict. For example, Mafatu has many hair-raising adventures (e.g., with sharks, storms), but all these incidents arise out of the main conflict and the boy's attempt to resolve it.

You might conclude the activity by asking partners or small groups to tell about conflicts in other stories, using a visual like the one above but leaving out the book title, the character's name, and setting details. Groups can then share and discuss visuals, guess which stories they refer to, and supply the missing information.

Conflict Brainstorm: A No-You-Can't

To further build the concept of story conflict, play a few rounds of No-You-Can't-Because. Here's how: Orally present a sentence or two stating "What I want to do." ("Whats" can be realistic or fanciful.) Have students brainstorm different reasons "Why you can't." (You might jot the ideas on poster paper to make an idea bank for future use.)

Examples:

1. **Teacher:** I want to raise St. Bernard dogs. What might *conflict* with what I want? That is, why can't I?

   Students:

   ❀ You can't because your apartment is too small!

   ❀ You can't because your mom is afraid of dogs!

   ❀ You can't because the super won't allow pets!

2. **Teacher:** I want to take a year-long trip around the world. Why can't I?

   Students:

   ❈ You can't because you might lose your teaching job.

   ❈ You can't because you don't have enough money.

   ❈ You can't because your family needs you.

When students have caught on to the strategy, encourage them to make up their own "I wants…" and ask classmates to offer "You can'ts…." Conclude the session by pointing out that students have identified many conflicts. Discuss which conflicts might make good story ideas.

 Suggest that students free-write about something they want a lot and what stands in the way of their getting it. While many students will immediately think of some coveted material possession, you might also direct their attention to nonmaterial "wants": achievements, adventures, careers, friendships, family relationships. Some students may wish to read aloud what they've written to one or two classmates before filing their free-writes in their Journals.

The Plot Thickens: Complications

The bulk of most plots is made up of complications: the assorted actions that the character takes to try to resolve the conflict.

Most of your readers are probably able to identify plot complications in books they've enjoyed: they're "the exciting parts," "the parts where I got worried (angry, happy, satisfied, curious)."

In good stories, the complications are logically related to each other and to the conflict. We suggest that you have students focus on this logic in literature because it's the area in which they—as young writers—often "wander off." They may introduce incidents that have little to do with the plot, or they may leave out crucial complications that logically would lead to the resolution of the conflict. Following are some activities for helping students develop useful ideas about the complications element in plots.

USE CHAPTER HEADINGS

List the chapter titles from a book the class is familiar with. If your Literature Circles have carried out the Literature Circle Suggestion on page 53, you might enlist their ideas. After briefly reviewing with the class the basic conflict in the story as a whole, discuss the big event in the chapter. What's the complication? How does it relate to the conflict? Create a chart on the chalkboard like the one on the next page.

USE A VIDEOTAPE OF A MOVIE

As an example here, we're using *Fly Away Home*, but the procedure can be adapted to almost any good movie for kids.

Direct Students' Viewing to let them know what they should be looking for: the basic conflict, and the main events, or complications, that happen to resolve the conflict.

Preview the Film Yourself to decide on four or five critical stopping points where you can pause and discuss the following with students:

Pause 1: What's the big conflict? (A daughter resents her father and can't adapt to his way of life.) What are some examples of the conflict? (The daughter is lonely; she misses her mother; she thinks the father's flying machine is weird.)

Other Pauses: What events, or complications, happen as the characters try to solve the conflict? (Ask for events in sequence. Emphasize strong, specific verbs.) (In her loneliness, the daughter *raises* a flock of baby geese. A game warden *warns* that the geese are doomed. The father *seeks* a way to *help* his daughter. He *perfects* his flying machine. He *teaches* his daughter how to fly it. The girl *encourages* the young geese to *follow* her plane. She *develops* some trust in and respect for her dad.)

Stop the Film Before the Climax. Good films, like good books, have a *climax*: the key exciting event that resolves the conflict. For example, in the movie *Fly Away Home* the climax is the daring flight in which the daughter must lead her beloved geese to a bird refuge in North Carolina before a deadline. We suggest that you stop the film you're showing just before the climax (e.g., just before the plane and geese take off for the crucial flight). You can then use the rest of the film to illustrate climax and resolution.

ADAPT TEST-TAKING SKILLS

As you know, standardized tests often present a series of words or phrases and ask students "Which one does *not* belong?" You can adapt this format to help your students identify complications (actions and events) that directly relate to a conflict and to eliminate actions and events that have little or nothing to do with the conflict. Start with simple problems and move on to more difficult ones. Ask students to tell how they made their choices. Here are some examples (answers are underlined):

1. **(Easy)**

   Conflict: A boy wants a pet. His parents think a pet would be a lot of trouble.

   Complications: What event in this story *doesn't* tell about the conflict?

   (A) The boy brings home a goldfish and explains how little care a goldfish needs.

   (B) A homeless stray puppy comes to the back door. The boy begs his mother to let him keep the puppy.

   (C) The boy and his friends play softball.

   (D) The boy's parents argue about pets.

2. **(Average)**

   Conflict: A girl wants to be an actress. Her family wants her to be a lawyer or a doctor.

   Complications: What event *doesn't* tell about the conflict?

   (A) The girl takes her family to a play.

   (B) The girl and her friends go to a basketball game.

   (C) The girl's family invites a lawyer to dinner.

   (D) The girl gets a movie star's autograph.

3. **(Harder)**

   Conflict: Sam is afraid of horses. He's especially afraid of Flash, the big white mare his older brother, Eddie, brings home.

   Complications: What *two* events are most related to the conflict?

   (A) Eddie rides Flash across meadows and through woods.

   (B) While Eddie is away at college, Flash gets sick and Sam has to stay in the stable all night to take care of her.

   (C) Sam puts poultices on Flash's sore leg.

   (D) Sam goes to Eddie's college graduation.

4. **(Challenging)**

   Conflict: Stella wants her family to speak English at home. Her family wants to speak the language of their home country.

   Complications: What *two* events are most related to the conflict?

   (A) Stella's father reprimands her when she speaks English.

   (B) Stella's father shows her important events in Spanish-language newspapers.

(C) When a fire breaks out in the oven, Stella's mother throws water on the flames.

(D) <u>Stella and her father must tell firefighters how to reach their house.</u>

 Students can review books they're familiar with to find complications the main character experiences in trying to settle a conflict, then dramatize one of these complications for classmates. For example, the group might dramatize the scene in "All Summer in a Day" in which Margot tells what the sun is like and her classmates scoff at her description. Ask the audience to identify how the complication grows out of the big conflict in the story.

Climax and Resolution

In books and short stories, your students have followed literary characters as they face their conflict and grapple with related complications as they seek to settle the conflict. The final settlement of the conflict comes in the climax of the story, usually an event in which the characters have to make a Big Decision. After the climax, there's a finale, the resolution—usually briefly presented—in which all the characters adapt to the Big Decision in one way or another. Here are some ways to help students identify climaxes in literature and to apply their understanding to the stories they'll write.

LOOK TOWARD THE END OF THE STORY

Explain to students that the climax of a story comes near the story's end. Many exciting events, or complications, may have happened as the character tries to solve the conflict. But now, almost at the end of the story, there's going to be a Super Event in which the character or characters must finally make a decision, perform an action, or reach an understanding that grows out of all these complications: One way or another, the conflict is settled. You might show this visually via a "math problem," as in the following example.

SOLVE THE CONFLICT

Event 1 + Event 2 + Event 3 + **EVENT 4 = Plot**

EVENT 4 = Super Event + Big Decision = CLIMAX

CLIMAX = Conflict Solved

You can use this strategy to help students determine the climaxes in other stories.

Examples:

✤ In *The Talking Earth*, the climactic event is a hurricane: through all the events and complications that Billie Wind has experienced so far, she has learned how to listen to the earth. Will she use what she's learned to survive the hurricane? Will she decide from this Super Event that the old wisdom of her people, the Seminoles, has real-life value?

❀ In "All Summer in a Day," the climactic event is the brief appearance of the sun. This is the event in which the conflict between Margot and her classmates is solved: she's right and they're wrong.

DISCUSS LOGIC

Briefly discuss what story logic is: a situation or idea that makes sense based on all the facts that precede it. Readers usually feel angry or "tricked" if the story climax isn't logical. Present some silly, or illogical climaxes, and encourage students to tell why they don't fit in with the conflict and the complications of the story. Examples:

❀ Mafatu is rescued by a UFO.

❀ Billie Wind meets a talent scout who takes her to Hollywood.

❀ Margot turns into a superhuman and puts all her classmates to sleep with a ZAP gun.

If you've been showing a video (page 56), now's the time for students to view the climax of the film to determine how it solves the conflict and why it makes sense. For example, in *Fly Away Home* the climax is the daughter and father's flight with the young geese from Canada to a bird refuge in the United States. This is the Super Event that will solve the conflict between the girl and her dad: Does the father really know what he's doing? Can the daughter finally respect and love him completely? As a result of the successful rescue operation, the answer to both questions is yes, and the conflict is over.

RESOLUTION: WHEW! AND HOW DOES EVERYBODY FEEL?

The *resolution* confirms how all the main characters feel and what they do now that the conflict has been resolved. For most stories, the resolution can be restated briefly. Examples:

❀ Cinderella married the prince and became a princess. And she lived happily ever after.

❀ As he left the vineyard, the fox grumbled, "So what if I couldn't reach the grapes? They were probably sour anyway!"

❀ Mafatu reached home safely, and his people honored him and declared him a hero who had conquered the sea.

Ask partners to compose brief one- or two-sentence restatements of resolutions in stories they've read, then share the restatements with a larger group. The audience should listen or read to decide and discuss:

❀ Does this resolution make me feel that the story is now complete? Do I know how the main characters feel now that the conflict is over?

❋ Is there something else I'd like to add to this restatement?

 Students who have made preliminary plot stairs (page 51) might refer to this journal page now and make a companion page titled A Revision of My Plot. Challenge students to make a new plot stair in which they use the headings Conflict, Complications, Climax, and Resolution. Invite students to confer with you to discuss the proposed story and any "wrinkles" they'd like to iron out.

Challenge Activity: Use Reader's Explorer 3

This Reader's Explorer (page 65) provides a format for developing a story plot.

Students can carry out the activity independently or with a partner or small group. Your basic preparatory step is to discuss with students some basic situations that might be entered under CONFLICT. Examples:

❋ **Shall I tell or not tell?** A kid is worried that his or her best friend is doing a lot of shoplifting.

❋ **Should I try it or not try it?** A kid is afraid of deep water, but some friends want him/her to go swimming with them.

❋ **Is it a fake or is it real?** A man says that a UFO has landed in his backyard, and a neighbor decides to investigate.

❋ **Who gets to make final decisions?** The music teacher wants school orchestra members to play classical music for the PTA concert, but the orchestra members want to play top-40 songs.

Preview with students the other Explorer headings and prompts they'll respond to. Clarify the goal by pointing out the final task they'll be leading up to.

Write a Short Story

In this step, students will write a short story, giving special attention to plot and applying the understanding they've developed about how a plot is constructed.

As you explain the assignment, let students know that they have options as to what their goal is, and help them, through conferencing, to choose a goal that meets their needs. Explain that they will eventually assess their own story, according to the goal they've set for themselves.

❋ The goal can be a great plot alone. This is a sensible focus for beginning writers, for writers whose stories so far have shown "weak plots" (the And-

It-Was-All-Just-a-Dream crowd), or for experienced writers who, through their own self-assessments, know they want to hunker down to make their story plots more exciting.

�֍ The goal can be twofold. Students who are reasonably confident about their ability to develop character, or to develop setting, can set as their goal the combining of one of these elements with a well-developed plot.

✷ The goal can be the whole caboodle: writing a short story in which plot, character, and setting are all developed in detail. This goal will appeal to your most experienced writers and most enthusiastic readers.

Prewriting

Ask all students to pull together the work they've done in exploring plot. Examples:

✷ Plot stairs

✷ Free-Writes

✷ Picture panels

✷ Journal entries

✷ Ideas from Literature Circles

✷ Diagrams and charts

✷ Notes about videos

✷ Completed Reader's Explorer 3

Students who've set themselves the goal of developing plot along with character and/or setting may wish to review their materials about these literary elements, too.

Ask students to group items that seem to begin a good "recipe" for a story. See example on the following page.

Next, ask students to fill in a paragraph frame that names the main characters in their proposed story, identifies the conflict, and states the first complication that happens because of the conflict. This prewriting strategy will get most students rolling. But assure students that they can change their plan as they draft their story. The frame follows. (Sample entries are shown in parentheses.)

The main characters in my story are <u>(Selena and a big stray dog named Max.)</u>
characters' names

The conflict is that <u>(Selena is afraid of dogs, but</u>
<u>Max is looking for a home.)</u>
conflict

The first complication is that <u>(Max follows Selena home and sits on the</u>
<u>doorstep. Now Selena's afraid to go outside!)</u>
first complication

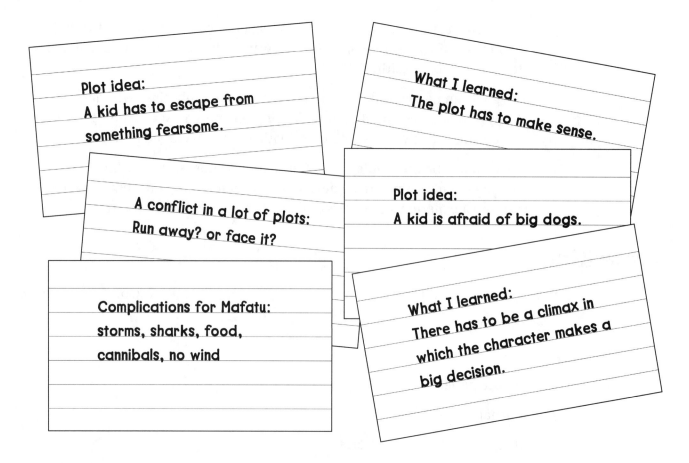

Plot idea:
A kid has to escape from something fearsome.

What I learned:
The plot has to make sense.

A conflict in a lot of plots:
Run away? or face it?

Plot idea:
A kid is afraid of big dogs.

Complications for Mafatu:
storms, sharks, food, cannibals, no wind

What I learned:
There has to be a climax in which the character makes a big decision.

Drafting

Allow at least two writing periods on consecutive days for students to draft their stories: almost all writers need some time to let a story "perk" and develop in their imagination and to reflect on how they've begun and how they might continue.

After the first writing session, the class might get together, with you as the moderator, to discuss any problems they may be encountering as they draft their stories. Stress that this is <u>not</u> the time to tell the story aloud or share drafts. (Telling a story aloud prematurely usually deflects the energy and motivation for writing it!) Instead, the class can pool and respond to general concerns, as in the following dialogue:

TEACHER: Sometimes I have a story all set in my mind, but when I sit down to write it, I wonder, "Well, exactly *how* shall I begin? Should I start with describing the characters, or the setting, or a big event?" Do any of you have a problem like that? What are some ways of solving it for the time being in your rough draft?"

Sample responses: Just start with the first thing that comes to mind. After all, this is just a *draft.* You can always change it later. Look at your prewriting notes. Choose the note that suggests the easiest thing to write about first. Think about the goal you've set for yourself. For example, if developing a great plot is your main goal, you could start with an event. If your goal is to concentrate on plot + character, you could emphasize what a character is *doing* as the story opens.

For your students who are primarily visual thinkers, suggest that they imagine their story as a movie, a play, or a TV drama, sketch the opening scene, then use the sketch as a picture-to-words prompt.

The best encouragement you can give to your writers is "Just keep going! Don't stop now to correct and change your story. You'll have time to do that when you revise."

Revising

Have each student make a copy of the draft for his or her writing partner. Then suggest these steps:

1. **Writer:** Before you give the copy to your partner, share the draft by reading it aloud. As you read, note on your own copy the parts that you like best and the parts you think need strengthening. (Writers might use pencils of two different colors to signal these parts.)

2. **Partner:** As you listen, note

   ❀ the parts of the story that you like best.

   ❀ the images or phrases that really stick in your mind.

   ❀ any questions you have about the plot: Do I know what the conflict is? Are all the complications related to the conflict? Is the conflict resolved in a way that makes sense to me?

3. **Writer and Partner Together:** Writers give partners the copy of the draft. The two discuss the questions above. The partner may wish to make suggestions for revising those parts of the draft that the writer has indicated "need strengthening." The writer may wish to respond to any cloudy elements of plot (conflict, complications, resolution) that have puzzled the partner. If the writer's own goal includes fully developing characters and/or setting along with the plot, the partners can also confer about how well this goal has been accomplished.

 In developing plots and revising their story drafts, writers can keep the reader (and themselves!) on track by using transitional words and phrases. This is an opportunity for you to teach or review some of these transitions. For each one, you may wish to provide a sample sentence, then ask students to use the transition in an original sentence.

Publishing

After students have made clean copies of their short stories, suggest that they choose at least two ways to publish them. Here are some options:

BOOKS

Students can illustrate, make covers for, and bind their individual stories. Small groups of students can share and discuss their stories. Or, the class can create a Short Story Anthology. Specific tasks to discuss and assign: front-cover art; title page; story illustrations; format (e.g., How shall we order the stories? Where will each story begin: on a right-hand or left-hand page? Where will the story illustrations be placed? Where will the author's name appear: at the beginning or at the end of the story?); table of contents; introduction; backcover material (some "teasers" about the stories? brief bios of the writers? excerpts from imaginary book reviews?).

For families and other away-from-school audiences, students might publish a Short Story Highlights Magazine, giving a great paragraph or two from each student's story. You might want to work with students to draft an introductory article which explains what they've learned about reading and writing stories.

DRAMA AND OTHER ORAL PRESENTATION

Groups of students can develop and present a play based on a classmate's story or present the story via Reader's Theater. Individual students may enjoy taping their own dramatic reading of their story (Caution: lots of practice first!) for classmates to enjoy independently or to take home to share with their families. Writers might also read their stories aloud to younger students in your school, then report to classmates about what the young audience enjoyed most and what the writer learned from the experience.

Reader's Explorer 3:
DESIGN A PLOT

Name _____

Date _____

BRAINSTORM:

1. What is the *conflict*?	2. What *complications* might happen	3. What might the *climax* be?
_____	A. _____	_____
_____	_____	_____
_____	AND	_____
_____	B. _____	_____
_____	_____	_____
_____	AND	OR MAYBE
_____	C. _____	_____
_____	_____	_____
	AND	_____
	D. _____	_____
	_____	

Go over your *complications*. Do they show events in sequence? Are they exciting? Do they all relate to the conflict? Are there any that don't? Make any changes that you wish.

Go over your two possible *climaxes*. Circle the one that is most exciting and really solves the conflict logically. Make changes if you wish.

Draft a one- or two-sentence *resolution* for your plot. Tell how your main character feels or acts now that the conflict is settled.

_____

_____

TELL YOUR STORY ALOUD TO SOME CLASSMATES: Use your Reader's Explorer as your storyteller's outline. Then ask for feedback: What did your audience like best? What questions do they have?

Expanding the Reading and Writing Experience

By doing the activities in the previous sections—Characters, Setting, Plot—most of your students will grasp the essentials of these three pivotal literary elements. As students continue to develop as writers and as critical readers, you may sense points when they're ready to fine-tune their understanding of "how stories work." This section presents ideas for exploring Point of View, Dialogue, Atmosphere and Imagery, and Theme.

Point of View

A good story is usually told from one standpoint. That is, the writer chooses a *point of view* and sticks to it throughout the story. Following are the most common points of view.

The All-Knowing (Omniscient) Point of View

The narrator, or storyteller, knows what **all** the characters are thinking and doing. Example:

> Over in the cowshed, Moo Maple was chewing her cud and wondering where her calf Elmore had gone. Meanwhile, Elmore was down by the pond with the ducklings. He had followed them there hoping to get some hints about swimming. The ducklings quacked gleefully: they liked having Elmore around. But Madam Duck quacked irritably. Twelve ducklings were enough of a burden, she thought, without having a clumsy calf to tend!

DISCUSS In presenting this example, ask students: Whose feelings, thoughts, and actions do we find out about? (the cow's, the calf's, the ducklings', the duck's). Explain why this is an example of the all-knowing point of view.

ACTIVITY Invite students to continue the story creating another paragraph that uses the all-knowing point of view. Students can compose orally, as a group, or write independently or with a partner. As students share their paragraphs, ask the audience to note what characters' actions and feelings are revealed and how students have developed different ideas for continuing the story.

The First-Person Point of View

The narrator is a character in the story and uses *I*, *me*, and so on to refer to herself or himself. From this point of view, readers only know what the *narrator* does, thinks, observes, and feels. Example:

> I thrashed my way through the underbrush, looking for a trail, a clue, anything that would help me find my sister. Where had she gone so suddenly, I wondered. Along with the panic, I felt anger. Krissy was always playing tricks on me! I could just imagine her saying to me, "Yah, yah, Mark! Fooled you again!" If this was a joke, too, I'd never forgive her.

DISCUSS In presenting this example, ask "Who's telling this story?" (Mark) How do you know? Who do *I*, *me*, *my* refer to?" Explain why this is an example of the first-person point of view. Ask why the first-person narrator can't tell us about Krissy's thoughts and feelings.

ACTIVITY Suggest that students choose an entry from their Journals or one of their free-writes, and shape it into a narrative paragraph told from the first-person point of view.

The Third-Person-Limited Point of View

The narrator is outside the story, but tells the story chiefly from the main character's point of view. The main character (e.g., Mafatu, Billie Wind) is the one whose actions, thoughts, and feelings the narrator concentrates on and tracks. While this point of view is the one used in most stories your students read, it's also one of the most difficult for writers to maintain. So don't expect "mastery."

DISCUSS Have students reread the excerpts from *Call It Courage* (page 22–23) and *The Talking Earth* (pages 24–25). Ask: From whose point of view are we *mainly* experiencing the sea? (Mafatu's) the weather and wildlife in the Everglades? (Billie Wind's).

ACTIVITIES 1. Present the two paragraphs that follow, and ask students to determine from whose point of view the stories are told.

A. (Point of view: Mafatu's mother)
Kuma had started out with her toddler son, Mafatu, in the hope of showing him the beauty of the sea, the sea's strength and riches. Now, as Kuma looked up into the billowing clouds, she knew that she and the child were in trouble. She clasped the little boy tightly to her, and struggled to get back to shore.

B. (Point of view: Charlie Wind's)
"Whatever can I say to convince this child?" thought Charlie Wind. He had always been proud of his niece, proud of Billie's courage and curiosity and energy. But now the girl was defying the beliefs that Charlie knew were important. He wondered what he could do to show her that Seminole beliefs made great sense.

2. Present the following paragraph, in which the point of view is third-person-limited, with the narrator focusing on the dog Max's feelings and actions. Ask students to work together to rewrite the paragraph to make it third-person-limited from the girl's point of view.

Max was hungry and tired and thoroughly lost. He had been shooed away, yelled at, and had stones thrown at him. Now here was this pleasant looking girl walking along with some delicious thing in that lunch box. It smelled like bologna, or maybe tuna fish. He wished the girl would stop. Was she afraid of him? She kept looking back at him with that Fear Look humans get sometimes. Well, Max was aware that he didn't look particularly great: his fur was matted, his ribs stuck out, and his left ear was still bleeding. Besides that, the girl was very little, and he was very big. But he kept plodding along after her, growling his message: "Hey, let's be friends!"

Sample rewrite:
Marisa looked back and saw the dog following her. He was huge and determined-looking. And that bloody ear! Marisa thought, "He must be fierce! Probably an attack dog!" Marisa decided to walk slowly, to pretend she wasn't

afraid. She clutched her lunch box, with its leftover sandwich, and walked on toward home. She could hear the dog growling behind her, and when she looked back again she noticed how matted his hair was, and how all his ribs stuck out, like he hadn't eaten in a long time. "Maybe he wants my sandwich," she thought.

ADDITIONAL ACTIVITIES

1. Invite Literature Circles to identify stories and novels that are written from different points of view. (See the Bibliography for suggestions.) The first-person point of view is pretty obvious. If students have differences of opinion about all-knowing and third-person-limited, encourage debate: the difference is not always cut-and-dried, and overlaps are possible. For example, *Charlotte's Web* certainly centers on Wilbur's activities and feelings and shows the world from his angle (third-person); yet the narrator also tells us what other characters—especially Charlotte—are thinking and doing (all-knowing).

   For your Literature Circle students, the aim is not to reach immovable opinions but to recognize point of view as a literary element that writers must think about as they work on their stories.

2. Student can have fun rewriting fairy tales and folktales from different points of view. The examples that follow are based on the story of Cinderella.

   ❋ Retell the story from a first-person point of view. Example:

   An Entry From Cinderella's Diary
   Dear Diary:
   What a life I lead! Scrubbing, cleaning, cooking! And now I have to help my stepsisters make dresses for the King's ball! How rude and awful these girls are! Don't they know how much I would like to go to a party once in a while?

   ❋ Retell the story from the third-person point of view, focusing on another character in the story. Example:

   The Godmother's Story
   Godmother Drusilla sat on her cloud, watching all her godchildren down below. Many of them were faring very well in the world. But then there was poor Cinderella! Drusilla worried about her a lot. She seemed to need some help. Drusilla wondered what she could do to help Cinderella escape from a life of drudgery.

3. Visually oriented students may enjoy making a picture panel that shows a scene from different observation points. For example, a picnic scene can be shown from the visual vantage points of a child eating a sandwich, a hungry ant, and a bird hovering high over the picnic area. After students have shown their panels and discussed them with classmates, suggest that they choose a writing partner and develop captions that describe the scene from the different vantage points.

Dialogue

Dialogue consists of the conversations characters have with one another. In well-wrought stories, dialogue has two main functions:

- It tells a lot about the characters' personalities.
- It moves the plot, or action, along.

Play scripts provide a good introduction to both uses of dialogue. On page 74, you'll find a script that presents characters and sets a plot in motion. Make and distribute copies of the script. Then use the following ideas.

Dialogue and Characters in a Play Script

INTRODUCE

Point out four facets of the script: *who* speaks, *how* they speak, *what* they say, and *how* the next character responds. Invite students to form acting groups and play the parts. Encourage them to build on what they've learned from the previous cast's renditions.

DISCUSS After a couple of run-throughs, ask: "What is each of these characters *like*? How would you describe their personalities? How do you know what they're like?" Point out to your students that their responses are based on the *dialogue*, or words, of the characters, and the *stage directions* (in capital letters), which tell how the character says the words and sometimes how the character behaves while speaking. (Students may wish to act out the script again after this discussion.)

ACTIVITIES 1. First, review with students that in stories, the dialogue—the exact words of a character—is shown within quotation marks; the writer may add words or phrases that show how the speakers say the words and what they do or feel while speaking. Examples:

- (from *The Talking Earth*)
  "Two lightning bolts?" she said with astonishment. "I can't do that."
- (from "All Summer in a Day")
  "Nothing!" he cried. "It was all a joke, wasn't it?" He turned to the other children. "Nothing's happening today. *Is* it?"
- (from *Call It Courage*)
  "We're going away, Uri," he whispered fiercely. "Off to the south there are other islands..."

Then, ask partners to find dialogue in stories the class has read and share this dialogue with other groups. What does the dialogue tell about the characters?

2. Challenge students to translate the play script to show how it might appear in story form. Example:

"I saw it! I saw it!" hollered Jake, jumping up and down with excitement.

Molly was bored with Jake's outbursts. "Oh, Jake," she sighed, "what are you freaking out about *now*?"

Dialogue and Plot in a Play Script

The sequence of dialogue in a play or story not only tells about character but also moves the plot along. That is, dialogue must be *relevant* to the plot: the words that characters speak should not only reveal their own personalities but also have something to do with the conflict and complications with which they're all involved.

DISCUSS Talk about the play script. What is the conflict? (Jake and Marisa think there's a ghost in the school; Molly and Mr. Jimez think this is nonsense.) How does the dialogue (the characters' words) tell about the conflict? (Examples: Marisa and Jake tell about what the ghost looks like and how long it's been prowling; Molly and Mr. Jimez try to convince otherwise.) Ask students: "Is there any dialogue here that does *not* relate to the conflict?" (No.)

ACTIVITIES 1. By practicing the test-taking skill of identifying what does not belong, students can determine what piece of dialogue would *not* further the plot of *A Ghost in Our School?*. Write the choices on the chalkboard. Call on students to read them aloud—as in a play—and ask the audience to tell (a) which dialogue does *not* belong (underlined below) and why not; (b) which dialogue *does* belong and why.

Example A:

(1) **MR. JIMEZ:** If there's really a ghost around, I'll help you find it!

(2) **MARISA:** <u>My brother's afraid of fire-engine sirens.</u>

(3) **MOLLY:** If you guys find a ghost, I'll give you all my lunch desserts for the next month!

Example B:

(1) **JAKE:** Well, hold my hand, Marisa! Because I don't like searching all these empty classrooms!

(2) **MARISA:** Do you hear that thumpety-bump, that peculiar whine?

(3) **MR. JIMEZ:** <u>Jake, I've been wanting to talk to you about your Science-Fair project.</u>

Example C:

(1) **MOLLY:** We didn't get the posters hung, Miss Morrison, because Jake and Marisa thought they saw a ghost.

(2) **MOLLY:** Miss Morrison, I have an idea for us Latch-Key kids: looking for ghosts in the school!

(3) **MOLLY (TO HERSELF):** I could put a sheet over my head and **boo** like some scary thing.

(4) **MOLLY (TO HERSELF):** <u>After my Dad comes for me at 5 o'clock, maybe we'll go to a movie.</u>

2. Ask students to form small groups to continue and complete the story *A Ghost in Our School?* Groups can use a play-script format or write a short story that uses a lot of dialogue to move the plot along. Oral presentations can consist of an acting-out of the script or a read-aloud of the story. Ask the audience to listen so that they can comment, in a follow-up discussion, about dialogue that relates to the plot and dialogue that doesn't.

3. Have students explore and share passages from literature where dialogue not only reveals character but also moves the plot along. For example, in the following dialogue from *The Talking Earth*, readers not only sense the differences between Billie Wind and her sister Mary but also get a clue that Billie is going to have some adventures that help her know "more than facts." (In the excerpt, Billie is the first speaker.)

"Why did you tell Charlie Wind on me?"

"Because you are too scientific. You are realistic like the white men."

"I see what I see. What I don't see, I don't believe."

"You were not that way before you went to the school at the Kennedy Space Center when our father worked for the scientists."

"That's not true. I've always been curious. I want answers, not legends. What is the matter with that?"

"What is the matter with that? I'll tell you. Someday you will be the head of your family and you'll need to know more than facts."

Invite students to translate these literary passages of dialogue into play form and present them as Reader's Theater to their classmates.

A PLAY BEGINNING

PLAY TITLE: *A Ghost in Our School?*

CHARACTERS: Molly, Jake, Marisa, Mr. Jimez
SETTING: A school hallway, 4 P.M.

JAKE (JUMPING UP AND DOWN EXCITEDLY):
I saw it! I saw it! I saw the ghost!

MOLLY (BORED):
Oh, Jake! What are you freaking out about now?

MARISA (LOOKING SCARED):
Oh, Molly, there IS a school ghost! It's a thing! A thing
all in gray that prowls the halls after school has let out!

JAKE (WORRIED):
It's been here for years! It was here when my sister Lucy
went to school here!

MARISA (SHIVERING):
It haunts the halls! My cousin told me so!

**MR. JIMEZ (LOOKING IRRITATED,
WALKING TOWARD THE STUDENTS):**
Exactly *what* are you kids doing out here in the hall?
Aren't you supposed to be in the After-School Latch-Key Room?

MOLLY (SOUNDING EXASPERATED):
Well, Mr. Jimez, we were sent out to hang posters in the hallway, but
then these guys got *hysterical* about some stupid ghost-thing!

MR. JIMEZ (PATIENTLY):
Now let's just investigate this. We'll explore the whole school and
look for this ghost of yours!

JAKE AND MARISA TOGETHER (REAL SCARED):
No, no, no, no!

MR. JIMEZ (SMILING):
Yes, yes, yes! We'll start in the cafeteria.

MOLLY (HEADING BACK DOWN THE HALL):
Count me out! I'm going back to the After-School Room! I don't
want anything to do with a silly ghost-hunting expedition.

Atmosphere and Imagery

Atmosphere is the prevailing mood in a piece of literature. Imagery is the sensory language and the metaphors that the writer uses to create that atmosphere.

Start With Atmosphere

Though atmosphere is the end result of lots of good word choices, it's a useful concept for students to consider first here. As readers they've already been using words that describe a book's atmosphere. For example, they're describing atmosphere when they say: "I like scary books." "A lot of mysterious things happen in Edgar Allen Poe's stories." "Harriet the Spy is mostly funny, although there are a couple of sad events, too."

DISCUSS An effective way to introduce the term atmosphere is to compare it to the feeling you get when you walk into a room. Ask students to close their eyes and imagine a classroom that has a happy atmosphere. What colors and objects do they see? What sounds do they hear? What are the students and teacher doing? List students' ideas on the chalkboard. Then repeat the sequence to create another atmosphere—for example, sad or mysterious. Talk about how a reader, as she or he "enters" a story, also picks up an atmosphere.

ACTIVITIES 1. Some students will enjoy painting pictures of the "atmosphere" they just described. Encourage them to make their pictures big and to use color and details to create the atmosphere. As students share their paintings, ask the audience to identify the atmosphere and tell what pictorial details develop it.

   As students respond, you may wish to jot down precise words and phrases that they use. Then give the list to the artist and suggest that she or he use them in a caption for or poem about the picture.

2. Ask partners or small groups to study familiar books to find passages that create a strong atmosphere and to identify the atmosphere with one or two words. For example, in Call It Courage, the paragraph beginning "Mafatu would never forget..." creates an atmosphere of dread, suspense, danger, or excitement. A group spokesperson can read the paragraph aloud to the class and tell why the group chose it.

Move On to Imagery

As they've studied the ways in which Character and Setting are developed, your students have had several experiences in identifying and using strong, precise descriptive words. Now they can move on to seeing that writers choose these words very consciously in order to create a particular atmosphere.

DISCUSS Review the term *imagery* with students. As it applies to literature, imagery is the use of words and phrases that appeal to our senses. Using a chalkboard chart, choose three or four familiar objects or experiences and ask students to suggest words and brief phrases that they might use to nail down sensory impressions. Example:

IMAGERY

Object or Experience	Sight	Hearing	Touch	Taste	Smell
ice-cream cone	a triangle of brown and white		cold, drippy	sweet	vanilla
swimming	green water	splash, holler	warm, gentle	salty	fishy
a candle	a moving flame on a white stalk	the "hss" when I light it	hot!		wax melting

Invite students to create imagery by composing oral sentences that use some of the words on the chart. Encourage a variety of sentences, and write them down. Examples:

❀ When I go swimming, I like the splash that the waves make and the taste of salt on my lips.

❀ The green water makes me holler with joy.

❀ I didn't like the fishy smell, but the warm and gentle touch of the water made up for it.

Discuss with students how their imagery makes the experience vivid to their audience. For example, why are the sentences above more interesting than simply "I like to go swimming"?

ACTIVITIES 1. On the chalkboard, present a bare-bones paragraph like the one that follows. Ask students to work in small groups to rewrite the paragraph so that it includes *imagery*. Before they begin to write, each group should decide what atmosphere they want to create through the imagery. For example, will the atmosphere be threatening? comfortable? amusing? magical? sad? Each image that the group chooses should build the atmosphere they've selected. (A sample rewrite follows the bare-bones paragraph.)

Bare-Bones
The prince approached the castle. Guards stood on the castle turrets. The drawbridge was down, and the prince walked across it. The moat below was deep. He heard sounds coming from the main hall.

Sample Rewrite. Atmosphere: Comfortable

The prince whistled as he approached the castle. Chattering guards waved from the castle turrets. The old, familiar drawbridge was down, and the prince strolled across it. The deep moat below reflected the flickers of stars. The prince heard laughter and music flowing out of the main hall.

Invite groups to read their rewritten paragraphs aloud to the class. Ask the audience to listen for and discuss the imagery that creates a particular atmosphere.

2. Ask students to pair-off with a classmate who likes the same kind of book, e.g., scary, adventurous, or funny. Partners choose a book they've both read, find a passage in the book that highlights the literary atmosphere they enjoy, then make a copy of the paragraph and underline the imagery that creates the atmosphere. One partner can read the paragraph aloud to the class; the other partner can ask classmates to identify the images that build the atmosphere.

Move On to Metaphor

A *metaphor* compares things that factually aren't really the same but that share some common characteristic. Examples:

"The *moon smiled* down at the *sleeping town*"
(The moon and the twon are compared to living things that can smile and sleep.)

Some of your students may already have explored metaphor through the activity on page 41. Here's another way to approach the concept:

DISCUSS   Create a web on the chalkboard. Start by writing "The girl danced" in the center of the web (page 78). Ask students to brainstorm sentences in which the verb (dance) might be used to tell about nonhuman things. Possible sentences are given on the following page.

Explain to students that the web they've completed consists of metaphors, or comparisons. Through metaphors, they've shown how one thing (e.g., a new idea, sunlight, a playful kitten) is like another (a human dancer) in some important way.

ACTIVITIES 1. You can help students practice a test-taking skill (which item *does not* belong) as they determine which metaphor *doesn't* belong in the creation of a certain atmosphere. Present these items. (Unrelated choices are underlined.) Ask students to identify the "wrong choice" and to explain why it doesn't develop the atmosphere.

(A) Atmosphere: Scary
    (1) The wind was a howling beast.
    (2) Sleet clawed at the windows.

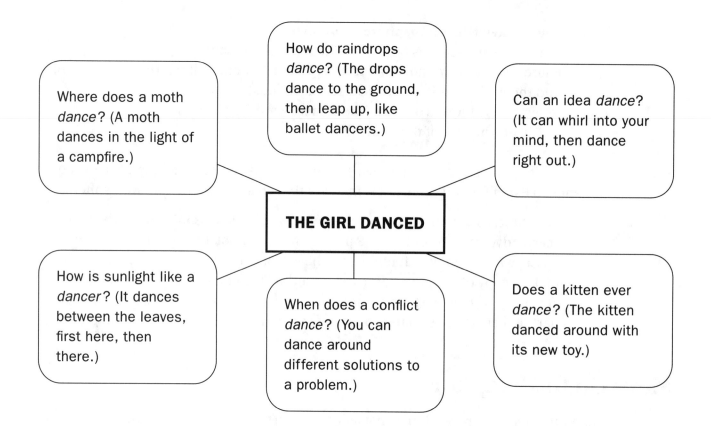

- (3) The lamp flickered in alarm.
- (4) <u>The music was a comfortable friend.</u>

(B) Atmosphere: Funny
- (1) "Hah!" said the stone, tripping Gallagher as he fell over it.
- (2) Miranda stumbled after him, floundering like a wobbly newborn colt.
- (3) <u>Huge, warped trees reached out for her, trying to capture her in their hungry limbs.</u>
- (4) Splat! Into a puddle! The water rippled, chuckling, "I told you so!"

(C) Atmosphere: Eerie
- (1) The sullen sun looked angry as it set.
- (2) <u>The perky, merry voice of the carousel invited her to the fair.</u>
- (3) Mist, like a gray cape, fell over her shoulders.
- (4) A shy, frightened breeze whispered, "Beware!"

After they discuss the metaphors that contribute to atmosphere, some students may wish to incorporate discussion ideas into a story of their own.

2. Ask reading partners to find three or four examples of metaphor in books they've enjoyed together. As they present their examples to classmates, partners should tell what is being compared to what. Examples (from *Call It Courage*):

"Night closed down upon them, swift as a frigate's wings..." (The sudden coming of night is compared to the fast movement of a bird's wings.)

"The sea muttered its eternal threat..." (The sound of the sea is compared to a person saying something scary.)

Theme

Theme is the major idea or ideas that a writer presents about life in general through the vehicle of the story. Discovering the theme(s) is usually the reader's task, because in most stories the writer doesn't state the theme conveniently in so many words. Instead, the reader has to put the story ideas and events together to come up with an overall "message" about life. Readers bring their own special backgrounds to their understanding of a story, so they may, accordingly and correctly, focus on and identify different themes in the same literary work.

Young readers often confuse *subject* and *theme*. For example, if you ask what the theme is in *My Side of the Mountain* or *The Talking Earth* or *Call It Courage*, many kids are likely to respond with a general phrase about the subject of the story, e.g., "living in the mountains," "exploring the Everglades," "surviving in the sea." While these responses may aptly sum up the subject of the story, they don't touch on the overarching ideas that allow readers to compare one story with another and to connect literature to their own lives.

Theme may be an initially difficult concept, but the following ideas can help your student begin to grasp and use it.

DISCUSS Literary themes are stated in sentences, not in one word or phrase. Present thematic statements (examples follow), and ask students to name books and stories that have that theme.

> Theme: By living with nature, we learn a lot about the world and about ourselves.
> Examples: *Banner in the Sky* (Ullman), *The Sign of the Beaver* (Speare), *The Talking Earth* (George)

> Theme: Solving family problems involves love and compromise.
> Examples: *Ida Early Comes Over the Mountain* (Burch), *The Summer of the Swans* (Byars), *Home from Far* (Little)

> Theme: A friendship is sometimes tested by tough lessons and decisions.
> Examples: *Me and the Terrible Two* (Conford), *Number the Stars* (Lowry), *Soup and Me* (Peck)

Also discuss how a story—especially a novel—may have more than one theme. For example, Speare's *The Sign of the Beaver* also develops the friendship theme stated above.

ACTIVITIES

1. Ask Literature Circles to choose two books that have a similar theme and discuss how the theme is developed in different ways. Suggest that the group create a visual presentation of the theme and its development. They can use the visual as they share their ideas with other groups.

2. When you're reading a novel aloud to the class, pause now and then to comment on how the story's theme relates to your own life and is similar to the theme in another familiar book. For example, if you're reading Karen Cushman's *The Ballad of Lucy Whipple*:

   > "I can sympathize with Lucy! I can remember when my family and I had to move to a new home thousands of miles away. It can be awfully difficult to leave a familiar place and all the things you love there."

   > "Does this story remind you so far of *Journey Home*? It does me, because there's a similar theme: When you have to adjust to hardship, you find all sorts of strengths in yourself that you never knew you had!"

   Use your comments as a lead-in to a teacher-student dialogue to enable students to contribute their own examples—from books and from real-life—of the theme's universality.

3. When students are drafting book reports or planning oral book reviews, remind them to include a statement of the book's theme.

4. Keep in mind that even for most professional writers, the theme of a story evolves as the story is drafted. The writer E. M. Forster put this concept concisely: "How do I know what I think until I see what I say?"

   In your students' own narrative writing, you may not want to make a big issue of theme. For most students, accomplishing the goals of character development, vivid descriptions of setting, and a coherent plot are achievements enough.

   However, for fluent, eager writers, considerations of theme can help them pull the draft of a story together as they revise it. When these students are engaged as partners in reviewing and commenting on drafts of one another's stories, suggest that they state the theme they detect in the work. Example:

   > "I like this story because the theme applies to most people. You seem to be saying that it takes a lot of courage to be true to your own beliefs."

   Partners can point out story details that helped them reach conclusions about theme or suggest ideas that might make the theme stronger.

Name _____ Date _____

READER'S SURVEY

1. Do you think of yourself as a good reader?_____
What are your strengths and weaknesses as a reader?

_____

_____

2. What could you do to become a better reader? _____

_____

3. How do you think reading is different from listening or from watching a story in a movie or on TV?

_____

_____

_____

4. When you read a story, how aware are you of the following:

	Always Aware	Usually Aware	Seldom Aware
Who the main characters are			
How the setting affects the characters			
The main conflict the characters face			
The writer's use of descriptive words			
The way the plot is developed			

5. Does reading stories help you to write your own stories? Explain.

_____

_____

_____

Name _____ Date _____

MY READING LOG

MY ASSESSMENT OF THE BOOK.
Rate books on a scale of 1 (not so good) to 5 (absolutely great). Then explain your rating by commenting on the literary elements.

1.

Title: _____

_____

Author: _____

_____

Rating: _____

Characters:

Setting:

Plot:

2.

Title: _____

_____

Author: _____

_____

Rating: _____

Characters:

Setting:

Plot:

3.

Title: _____

_____

Author: _____

_____

Rating: _____

Characters:

Setting:

Plot:

READER'S SURVEY:

Ideas for Organizing Your Readers-as-Writers Journal

Organize with CATEGORY HEADINGS. Remember that you can always:

- ⸙ reword headings, combine them, delete them, or add more.
- ⸙ move journal pages around.

1. FOR BOOKS YOU'RE READING: Place your journal entries, free-writes, Literature Circle notes, and any pictures you draw in the general category where you think they belong. Examples of categories:

- ⸙ CHARACTERS AND CONFLICTS
- ⸙ INTERESTING SETTINGS
- ⸙ PLOT STEPS IN MY FAVORITE BOOKS
- ⸙ WHAT I'VE LEARNED FROM CERTAIN STORIES
- ⸙ QUESTIONS I HAVE ABOUT HOW A STORY ENDS

2. FOR IDEAS FOR YOUR OWN STORIES: Using the same categories you've created for books you've read. Choose another color of paper or ink to signify ideas for your own stories.

GOOD SETTINGS!

Lit. Circle notes: *The Talking Earth* We picked out good descriptive words and phrases, like *soft trade wind, cooling the air pleasantly.*

A Setting for my story "A Distant Planet" Some descriptive words I might use: *mysterious fog, a scorching wind, yellow light flickering*

Name _____ Date _____

READER'S SURVEY:

Ideas for Presenting Your Journal

Select the journal entries that you think represent your very best ideas and questions about books and about your own stories. Attach comments that you'd like a classmate or your teacher to respond to as they read your journal entries. Here are some sample comment slips that one student used:

This book seems to have a lot of themes! I had some trouble figuring out the main theme. My ideas are attached.

Some stories give me ideas about my own life. Do they apply to your life, too?

I worked really hard on the plot for this story. Check to see if I
- show the conflict.
- make the plot sensible.
- show how the characters resolved the conflict.

Look through your journal. Find two or three entries you'd like to share. On the lines below, tell what you want a partner to notice about your entries.

_____

_____

_____

_____

_____

Name _____ Date _____

READERS-AS-WRITERS SURVEY

1. As a reader, what do you think are the most important qualities of a really great story?

_____

_____

2. As a writer of stories, what do you think your strengths are?

_____

_____

3. As a writer of stories, what do you think your weaknesses are?

_____

_____

4. As a story writer, how much attention do you give to the following:

	A Lot of Attention	Some Attention	Very Little Attention
Making the main characters different			
Showing what the conflict is			
Describing the story setting			
Constructing a plot that makes sense to readers			
Settling the conflict in a believable way			
Using imagery and metaphors to help readers see what's happening			

5. In the next story you write, what is your goal going to be?

_____

Partners' Names: Writer _____ Reviewer _____

GOING OVER THE DRAFT OF A STORY

REVIEWER: Fill in the chart with your ideas, observations, and suggestions. Then give your chart to your writing partner.

1. What I like best in your story:

2. Images or ideas that stick in my mind:

3. The main characters in your story seem to be:

4. As I see it, the main theme or point or lesson in your story seems to be:

5. I have some problems understanding the following:
(Circle the ones that apply.)

What the conflict is	Some steps in the plot	How the conflict is settled
Where the story takes place	What the characters are like	What the characters have learned at the end of the story

WRITER: With your partner, discuss the completed chart. Then use the chart and your discussion in any way you wish as you revise your story.

Name _____ Date _____

TEACHER-STUDENT CONFERENCE:

Student's Comprehension of Literary Elements

Story/Book:_____

ELEMENTS	UNDERSTANDING DEMONSTRATED	COMMENTS
Name the main characters.		
Name some other characters.		
Where and when does the story take place?		
What is the main character's problem or goal?		
What stands in the way that makes the problem hard to solve?		
What are some big steps the characters take as they try to solve the problem? (Ask the student to tell the plot steps in sequence.)		
How is the problem finally solved?		
How do the main characters feel or act now that the problem is solved?		
Does the main idea, or theme, in this story remind you of real-life situations in some way? How?		

Name _____ Date _____

TEACHER'S ASSESSMENT:

Student's Use of Literary Elements in Her or His Own Stories

LITERARY ELEMENTS	A FIRST STORY	A LATER STORY	COMMENTS
CHARACTER: • Names and distinguishes them clearly • Uses dialogue to delineate character • Reveals what a character is feeling			
SETTING: • Clearly indicates where and when the story takes place • Uses vivid words and phrases to create word pictures			
PLOT: • Makes clear what the central conflict is • Develops the plot in logical steps • Tells about the major decision that settles the conflict • Tells how the main characters act or feel when the conflict is settled			

Names _____ Date _____

_____

WAYS TO RETELL STORIES

There are several different ways to retell a good story. Try all or some of the ways. With your partner, fill in the chart to report on your retelling experiences.

RETELL:	The story title:	My partner's assessment of my work:	My self-assessment of my work:
LISTENING: Your partner reads the story aloud. YOU retell it by: **1.** Drawing pictures. **2.** Retelling the story aloud. **3.** Retelling the story in writing.			
READING: YOU read the story silently. Then you retell it to your partner by: **1.** Drawing pictures. **2.** Retelling the story aloud. **3.** Retelling the story in writing.			

Glossary of Literary Elements

ATMOSPHERE

Atmosphere is the general feeling or mood in a work of literature. Writers create atmosphere by using imagery and descriptions. Readers can usually describe atmosphere in just a word or two—for example, "a *scary* poem," "an *exciting* scene," "a story filled with *sadness*."

CHARACTER

A character is a person or an animal in a work of literature.

CHARACTERIZATION

Characterization is *how* the writer reveals what a character is like. Writers do this in different ways:

Direct Characterization: The writer simply tells what the character is like. Example: The goddess Aphrodite was tall, beautiful, and powerful.

Indirect Characterization: The writer gives the actual words of the character, tells what the character is thinking and feeling, tells about the character's actions, or tells how others respond to the character. Example:

> Aphrodite felt unhappy when she saw Echo crying. "I don't like to see you suffering so," the goddess said.

CLIMAX Climax is the exciting point in the story where the main character or characters face and make a huge decision. For readers the climax is usually the most suspenseful part of the story. It's the point where the conflict will finally be settled.

CONFLICT Conflict is the big struggle between characters or between opposing forces. A conflict may be *external* or *internal*. Some stories have both kinds of conflict.

External Conflict: The main character struggles with another person or with an outside force, like the sea.

Internal Conflict: The main character struggles with opposing ideas or feelings within his or her own mind, like wanting to be independent but also needing the approval of others.

DIALOGUE Dialogue consists of the exact words that characters say. When you write dialogue, you use quotation marks to enclose the exact words. Example:

> "Don't even try to climb that mountain!" said Luis.

> "Why not?" replied Shana. "I like challenges!"

IMAGERY   Imagery is language that appeals to the senses. Examples:

> a freezing-cold snow cone; the fragile and gentle touch of a butterfly's wings, the screeching cry of an owl

METAPHOR   A metaphor is a word or phrase that compares one thing to another. Metaphors are not factually true, but they help readers to see events and characters in a vivid way. Examples:

> The hurricane was *like a huge beast trying to devour us.*
>
> The wind *looked in at the windows and snarled.*

MOTIVATION

Motivation is *why* characters behave in a certain way. As a reader you can track motivation with *because* sentences. Examples:

> Mafatu ventures onto the ocean alone *because* he must prove that he can be a courageous seafarer.
>
> Billie Wind sets out alone into the Everglades *because* she wants to test Seminole beliefs.

PLOT   Plot is the series of related events that make up the story. Most plots go this way:

> The *introduction* tells who the main characters are and what the main conflict is.
>
> Complications develop as characters do things to try to solve the conflict.
>
> In the *climax,* the main characters make a final decision that solves the conflict.
>
> The story ends with a *resolution*: the writer tells what the main characters feel or do now that the conflict is over.

POINT OF VIEW

The point of view in a literary work is the vantage point from which the story is told. Two examples are the first-person point of view and the all-knowing point of view.

SETTING   Setting is the time and place in which story events occur.

THEME   Theme is the big idea that the story conveys about life. The writer usually doesn't state the theme directly. It's up to readers to discover the theme for themselves. When you've found the theme, you'll be able summarize it in a complete sentence or two. For example, the theme of *Call It Courage* might be "You can't be brave unless you know what it is to be afraid."

Bibliography

This bibliography includes stories cited in the activities as well other books—mostly recent, but some golden oldies, too—that we think might be particularly helpful to your students as they study and use the basic literary elements. Of course, there are hundreds of other great books that we are unable to list here. We suggest that you use this bibliography simply as a starting point. Add and annotate other titles that are among your favorites, and invite your students to do the same. Your class can then produce its own original Parade of Great Books, which can be shared with other students in your school or through your local library.

Aiken, Joan. *Cold Shoulder Road.* (Delacorte, 1996). Aiken continues the Gothic-novel story of Is, the heroine of *Is Underground* (Delacorte). Here Is, with her cousin Arun, moves through fantastic and dangerous settings in search of Arun's mother. The settings are a prime feature in this book, melding real histories of places with highly imaginative segues into fantasy.

Avi. *Beyond the Western Sea: Book One: The Escape From Home.* (Orchard, 1996). In this chapter book, chapters end with dilemmas that impel the reader to go on and on! How will Maura and Patrick—young victims of the Irish potato famine—find their way alone to the New World?

Caduto, Michael J., and **Joseph Bruchac.** *Keepers of the Earth.* (Fulcrum, 1988). These stories from many Native American cultures intimately involve characters with their natural surroundings. Basic plots grow out of this interaction between people and their settings. The stories provide especially good models for students who are interested in ecology or who have environmental concerns.

Choi, Sook Nyul. *Echoes of the White Giraffe.* (Houghton, 1993). During the Korean War, fifteen-year-old Sookan flees—with remnants of her family—from Seoul to a province in southern Korea. While the wartime setting of the book is powerfully presented, one of the story's principal values to your students may be as a model of literary conflict. Here, it's the age-old, universal conflict between young people and their families' traditional values. Sookan, who wants to become independent, must at the same time consider what her mother expects of her.

Clements, Andrew. *Frindle.* (Simon & Schuster, 1996). This is a funny novel built on the tried-and-true theme of the student-teacher battle. Nick, a chronic procrastinator, grapples with his match, Mrs. Granger, as he tries constantly to distract her with side issues, many of which are about language. (*Frindle* is Nick's new name for *pen.*) The dialogue is outstanding, establishing character and moving the plot along.

Cushman, Karen. *The Ballad of Lucy Whipple.* (Clarion, 1996). This is a great book for modeling the first-person point of view and also as an example of how plot events bring about changes in a character. Lucy, the narrator, has been swept out to gold-rush California by her pioneering family. She longs for her New England home and stubbornly digs in her heels when she's asked to "adjust" to her new surroundings. The challenges in this new environment, and the empathy Lucy develops for people who share it, eventually bring her around to a new concept of what "home" is and to an appreciation of her own coping abilities.

Farmer, Nancy. *A Girl Named Disaster*. (Orchard, 1996) The setting is Mozambique and Zimbabwe. The heroine is Nhamo, who seeks to escape an unfortunate, arranged marriage by setting off alone in a small boat to find haven with her father. When the boat drifts off course and Nhamo is stranded on an uninhabited island, she must summon up all her survival skills and rely, too, on the traditional teachings of her people. The setting is richly evoked, and the heroine is a believable model of courage and enterprise. As your students compare plots and characters, they might use this book along with other "survival stories" such as *Call It Courage, The Talking Earth, Sign of the Beaver, Island of the Blue Dolphins,* and *My Side of the Mountain.*

Fine, Anne. *Step by Wicked Step* (Little Brown, 1996). Theme is the star literary element in this novel. Being part of a stepfamily is disturbing and challenging. Five children who face this challenge find an ancient journal that deals with this problem. Reading and sharing the journal inspires the children to share their experiences and to work toward solutions.

George, Jean Craighead. *The Talking Earth*. (Harper Paper, 1983). The character of intrepid Billie Wind, the exciting setting of the Florida Everglades, and the "survival" plot are enough to keep most of your students turning the pages of this now-classic novel. In discussing this book, you might also want to focus on themes, such as how individuals have to reconcile their personal goals and ideas with those of their families and cultural groups and how only through testing yourself to the limit can you discover what your strengths are. These are favorite themes of the author, and students can also explore them through her *My Side of the Mountain* (Dutton, 1967) and *Julie of the Wolves* (Harper, 1972).

Hoestlandt, Jo. Translated by Mark Polizzotti. *Star of Fear, Star of Hope*. (Walker, 1995). Originally published in France, this is the story of the Holocaust as told by the fictional Helen, who recalls how her best friend Lydia and her family disappeared one night during the Nazi invasion of France in 1942. Johanna Kang's stunning illustrations won the Graphics Prize at the 1994 Bologna Book Fair.

Locker, Thomas. *Where the River Begins*. (Dial, 1984). Locker's art in this and in all his books is really "the story." His words expand and develop simple plots: here, with their grandfather, Josh and Aaron explore the source of the Hudson River. But it's the pictures that essentially evoke the setting and show the warmth and contact between the characters. Locker's book provides a good model for students who are primarily visual thinkers or for any student who gets story ideas from viewing fine art.

Mahy, Margaret. *The Door in the Air and Other Stories*. (Dell Paper, 1988). The nine short stories here range in tone from funny to gripping to thought provoking. While all the stories have "fantasy" settings and plots—and will thus appeal to students who favor that genre—they also all focus on kids' real-life concerns, such as sibling rivalry and parental expectations. Thus, you might use the stories as you discuss theme with your students.

O'Dell, Scott. *Island of the Blue Dolphins.* (Dell Paper, 1987). In this first-person narrative, Karana relates how she survived alone for 18 years on a deserted island in the Pacific Ocean. The book is notable for its matter-of-fact and explicit details about the setting and for the way it reveals Karana's character through what she *thinks* and *does.*

Philbrick, Rodman. *The Fire Pony.* (Blue Sky, 1995). The setting is a ranch. The plot, though anything but cheery, is gripping. The characters are so well wrought that you'll want to use them as models with your students. The first-person narrator, Roy, is the battered but valiant survivor of a dreadful foster home. Joe, Roy's brother, who has rescued Roy, is funny but also weird and unpredictable. Tension builds! Also use the book to focus on climax.

Reilly, Patricia. *Lily's Crossing.* (Delacorte, 1997). The setting is the USA "homefront" during World War II. Lily's comfortable life comes apart as the war carries away her father and her best friend and brings in an encounter with Albert, a Hungarian refugee. The climax of the story is especially good: Lily's tendency to tell lies involves Albert in a near tragedy as he rows out to sea to search for his sister.

Rylant, Cynthia. *The Van Gogh Cafe.* (Harcourt, 1995). Rylant's six short stories are built around supernatural events that take place in a Kansas cafe that was once a theater. The fun and enchantment are seen through the eyes of 10-year-old Clara, who runs the cafe with her father.

Siegelson, Kim. *The Terrible, Wonderful Tellin' at Hog Hammock.* (Harper, 1996). This is a great book to use as a read-aloud and to suggest to students who think they have "no stories to tell." The book's protagonist, Jonas, is upset because—when his grandfather dies—he has to take over the role of storyteller at the traditional "tellin'" at the Sea Islands in Georgia. Jonas finds that he has more stories to tell than he had ever imagined, and he also learns the value of oral history.

Soto, Gary. *Baseball in April.* (Harcourt, 1990). Soto's short stories, all simply told, manage to clearly delineate several different characters and to present a vivid picture of Latino culture in California. This is a good book to use when you want kids to focus on the social aspects of setting.

Speare, Elizabeth George. *The Sign of the Beaver.* (Houghton, 1983). Here's another "survival story" in a long-ago setting (pioneer New England). As your readers enjoy the exciting plot, you might call their attention to one of the themes that relates to their here-and-now life: To get along in life, you have to be open to ideas from people who are different from you. In Speare's book, both Matt and Attean learn from each other.

Sperry, Armstrong. *Call It Courage.* (Aladdin Paper, 1990). This story, first published in 1940, still stands as a prime example of a character facing a mighty conflict and moving through exciting settings and events to resolve the conflict. Mafatu—distant as he may be in time and place from most readers of his story—exhibits universal, timeless characteristics: fear, doubt, determination, enterprise, a yearning for acceptance, and a need to test oneself. There's a Mafatu in almost every one of your students.

Uchida, Yoshiko. *Journey Home.* (Atheneum Paper, 1992). The setting is California at the conclusion of World War II. The main character, Yuki, strives to get her life back in order after she and her family—Japanese Americans—have been released from Topaz, an internment (concentration) camp in Utah. The novel is remarkable in the way it presents setting (history, culture, and place). It's also a great model of how dialogue delineates character and keeps the plot moving.

Vail, Rachel. *Daring to Be Abigail.* (Orchard, 1995). Here's a model of how the main character *changes* through events and insights. Abigail, a popular member of a summer camp, reconsiders her priorities and sheds her self-absorption as she "rescues" a nerdy fellow camper from taunts and isolation.

Yolen, Jane, and Martin Greenberg and Charles G. Waugh, eds. *Dragons and Dreams: A Collection of New Fantasy and Science Fiction Stories.* (Harper, 1986). The stories in this collection—all by outstanding writers of fantasy and sci-fi—not only appeal to kids who favor these genres but also present fine models of how to integrate believable characters and plot into exotic settings.

Some Magazines That Often Publish Students' Writing

Students learn a lot about literature through enjoying and critiquing published work by their peers. Your school or local library may subscribe to the following periodicals or be able to acquire samples of them. Your students may also wish to submit some of their writing for possible publication in the magazines. This is your call, however. Confer with your students. Like all writers, young ones have to develop strong egos that let them accept "rejection slips" without taking it personally and without breaking their stride as they go on writing.

Addresses and phone numbers are those of the editorial offices.

Stone Soup
This bimonthly, 48-page magazine is made up exclusively of fiction, nonfiction, poetry, photos, and pictures by children ages 7–13. Children's Art Foundation, P.O. Box 83, Santa Cruz, CA 95063. Telephone: 800-447-4569.

Young Voices
Another bimonthly, this magazine welcomes fiction, essays, and poems that give a personal perspective on kids' views of the world. P.O. Box 2321, Olympia, WA 98507. Telephone: 206-357-4683.

Storyworks Magazine

This magazine features short stories, plays, poems, and nonfiction by top children's authors and provides a teacher's edition. *Storyworks* welcomes your students' book reviews and their letters about literature. Scholastic Inc., 555 Broadway, New York, NY 10012. Telephone: 212-343-6298.

Owl

Articles and stories here are aimed toward children ages 8+ who are interested in nature and science. The magazine publishes students' poetry and stories that reflect this focus. Young Naturalist Foundation, 56 The Esplanade Suite 306, Toronto, Ont., Canada M5E 1A7. Telephone: 416-868-6001.

The Acorn

This magazine has a very small circulation, but aims to be a beginning showcase for students' stories. 1530 Seventh Street, Rock Island, IL 61201. Telephone: 309-788-3980. (*Betty Mowery*)

Harambee

This bimonthly focuses on African and African American history and culture. Each issue has a theme, and students' stories are occasionally published. Just Us Books, Inc., 301 Main Street, Orange, NJ 07050. Telephone: 201-676-4345.

Creative Kids

Designed for an audience ages 8–14, this magazine stresses merit: striving for the best work you can do. It publishes kids' poems, short stories, mysteries, and photographs. Prufrock Press, P.O. Box 8813, Waco, TX 76714-8813. Telephone: 800-998-2208. #8 (*Libby Lindsey*)

Children's Digest

The audience is preteens, and the focus for readers is contemporary fiction. Student writers are invited to submit *very* short stories (maximum 200 words) and poems. Children's Better Health Institute, P.O. Box 567, Indianapolis, IN 46206. Telephone: 317-636-8881.

Highlights for Children

You're probably familiar with this activity-oriented magazine, which has a circulation of 3,000,000 and interests kids up to 12 years old. From time to time, *Highlights* publishes students' short-short stories (maximum 200 words). 803 Church Street, Honesdale, PA 18431. Telephone: 717-253-1080.